Anonymous

The Lyanough Cook Book

Anonymous

The Lyanough Cook Book

ISBN/EAN: 9783744781343

Printed in Europe, USA, Canada, Australia, Japan

Cover: Foto ©Lupo / pixelio.de

More available books at **www.hansebooks.com**

A RECIPE.

MEGATHLIN'S DRUG STORE as you know,
Always carries quite a show
Of Medicines to cure all ills,
From powders fine to Quinine pills.

The rarest sweets in town you'll find!
Huyler's! Foss' and the famous twenty-nine.
Soda! A wondrous drink indeed,
That ten-cent chocolate with cream.

Our spices did you ever try?
Pure and fresh for cake and pie.
Our flavorings are the very best,
Vanilla, Strawberry, and all the rest.

Prescriptions filled with greatest care,
At prices that are right and square.
There's nothing in the Druggist line
But what at MEGATHLIN'S you will find.

THE IYANOUGH COOK BOOK

SECOND EDITION, ENLARGED AND IMPROVED.

PUBLISHED BY THE LADIES OF THE

HYANNIS PUBLIC LIBRARY ASSOCIATION.

Price 25 Cents.

HYANNIS, MASS.
F. B. & F. P. GOSS, PUBLISHERS.
1899.

PREFACE.

The sale of the entire edition (five hundred copies) of the IVAN-OUGH COOK BOOK and the call for more, prove it a wage-earner for the library, and is the excuse for publishing a second, and enlarged edition.

To those who have responded to the call for recipes, the Association wishes to express its appreciation; also to the advertisers, whose patronage has largely defrayed the expenses of printing, etc.

MENU.

It is the bounty of nature that we live! but of philosophy that we live well.
—*Seneca.*

Soups and Chowders.

BROWN SOUP STOCK.—6 pounds hind shin of beef, 6 quarts cold water, 10 whole cloves, 10 pepper corns, 1 large tablespoonful salt, 3 small onions, 1 carrot, 2 stalks celery or 1-4 teaspoonful celery seed, 1 turnip, 2 sprigs of parsley. Wipe and cut the meat into pieces. Put the marrow bones and half the meat into the cold water in the kettle. Soak half an hour. Before heating, add spices and herbs, 2 teaspoonfuls mixed. Brown the onions and the remainder of the meat and add to the stock, then add the vegetables, cut fine. Simmer six or seven hours and strain. After taking off the fat, the next day clear with whites and shells of 3 eggs put in when cold. When it comes to a boil, let it cool for three minutes, then strain through a cloth.--[Mrs. E. F. Smith.

SOUP FROM BEEF EXTRACT.—1 teaspoonful of beef extract, 1 quart of boiling water, a small onion, 2 sticks of celery, half a teaspoonful of salt, a shake of pepper. Let all cook three-quarters of an hour and then strain.—[Mrs. E. F. Smith.

BEEF SOUP.—4 pounds beef, little more than cover with water, 3 onions, 1 teacup of rice, salt and pepper to taste.
—[Mrs. Ernest Harlow.

SHERRY BOUILLON.—4 pounds of juicy beef, 1 knuckle of veal, 2 small turnips, 2 carrots, 1 soup bunch, 1 small red pepper, 2 small white onions, salt, six quarts of water. Boil six hours and strain through a sieve. Let it stand over night, skim off the grease, put in a kettle to heat, and add sherry to taste.

—[Mrs. Sara T. Hammond.

LAMB SOUP.—2 pounds lamb, 2 quarts water, 4 medium spoonfuls of salt, little pepper. Cook one hour. Add 3-4 cup rice; add potatoes and turnips; add macaroni.

—[Mrs. Ernest Harlow.

MOCK TURTLE SOUP.—Take half a calf's head, remove the brain and skin, wash thoroughly, soak over night in salted water, boil until tender in two quarts of beef stock and two quarts of water, skim carefully. Take up the head, remove the bones, chop fine, set in a cool place; add to the liquor 1 onion, 1 carrot, 1 small turnip, 1 cup of chopped cabbage, a sprig of parsley, a few stalks of celery, a little mace, the grated rind of a lemon, a small bunch of sweet herbs, salt and pepper. Let simmer one hour, strain through cheese cloth, reheat, add a few fine bread crumbs, thinly sliced lemons, tablespoonful Worcestershire sauce, and a gill of port wine. The more it is warmed over the better it is.—[Mrs. F. I. Storer.

CREAM OF CELERY SOUP.—1 head of celery, cut fine, and 1 onion. Boil till soft. Put through a colander, add 1 quart boiling milk, 1 tablespoonful cornstarch, 1 tablespoonful butter, salt and pepper to taste. Boil a few minutes. Put 1-2 cup whipped cream in tureen and pour the soup over it.—[Mrs. C. E. Harris.

CELERY SOUP.—Delicious soup is made in this way: Boil a small cup of rice in a little over a quart of milk. Boil until it is so soft that it will pass through a sieve with but little effort on

your part. Grate the nicely bleached parts of 2 heads of celery, and add to the strained rice; add to this 1 quart of strong beef stock, or that made from mutton or veal may be used; it should be strained, and be clear and free from lumps when it is put in with the rice. Let this boil until the celery is tender. Season with a dash of cayenne pepper, or a little curry powder, and plenty of salt. If it is difficult to obtain celery when you wish to have this soup, celery salt may be used, or even celery seed or extract.
—[Mrs. W. A. Baldwin.

CAULIFLOWER SOUP.—Take the water in which a cauliflower has been boiled, add half as much milk and butter size of an egg, pepper and salt to taste, and thicken slightly. Serve very hot.
—[M. P. C.

MOCK BISQUE SOUP.—Place over fire 1 can of tomatoes. Stew until soft, then strain, and add 1-2 saltspoonful soda, returning to fire. Have ready 1 quart hot milk; to this add 1 tablespoonful cornstarch, dissolved in 1-3 of a cup of melted butter. Cook for ten minutes. Stir frequently. Add tomatoes, and season with salt and pepper. Serve very hot.—[Mrs. E. L. Chase.

TOMATO SOUP.—2 quarts milk, juice from 1 can tomatoes. Let milk come to a boil, put in tomato juice, and at same time a pinch of soda. Set back, put in a piece of butter, salt and pepper to taste. Avoid boiling.—[Mrs. Edwin Baxter, Jr.

POTATO SOUP.—Take cold meat and boil about one hour, then put in about a dozen potatoes, an onion, and half a bunch of celery if obtainable. Boil until the potatoes are cooked, then strain, put in parsley, chopped fine, and serve. This makes a cheap and healthy soup.—[Mrs. E. A. Baxter.

POTATO SOUP.—1 quart milk, 6 potatoes, 2 onions, 1-2 pint water, 1 tablespoonful parsley, 1-2 saltspoonful white pepper, or 1-4

8

teaspoonful black, 1 teaspoonful salt, 3 teaspoonfuls butter, 1 teaspoonful celery salt. Boil 6 large potatoes (peeled) with 2 onions. Have the milk and water hot, and put in it the potatoes and onions, mashed. A potato ricer is the better thing to use instead of a masher. Stir constantly so the soup will be smooth. When thickened a little, beat 1 egg very light, and put into the tureen; turn soup over it.—[Mrs. William Lovell, Jr.

GREEN CORN SOUP.—6 ears of sweet corn, water to cover the ears, 1 pint milk or cream, 1 teaspoonful salt, 1 teaspoonful each of sugar, flour and butter, 1-2 saltspoonful white pepper. Remove the pulp, leaving hull on the cob, cover with cold water and boil thirty minutes; after straining there should be a pint of water. To this add the pulp and boil fifteen minutes, then add salt, pepper, sugar and the boiling milk. Thicken with 1 teaspoonful flour and 1 tablespoonful butter, cooked together. Boil five minutes, and serve at once.—[Mrs. Henrietta E. Chase.

GREEN PEA SOUP.—2 quarts green peas, 1-4 pound butter, 2 small onions, a little parsley. Cook until tender in enough water to cover, add 2 quarts of stock, pepper and salt to taste, 1 large spoonful sugar. Let this boil once and strain through hair sieve, then add 1 pint of boiling milk and cook five minutes.

—[Mrs. C. A. B.

SPLIT PEA SOUP.—1 1-2 pounds peas; put to soak over night in 4 quarts of cold water. In the morning add a ham bone or a few salt pork ribs, an onion, 3 cloves, salt and pepper to taste. Cook until soft, strain through coarse sieve, and serve hot.

—[Mrs. F. I. Storer.

BEAN SOUP.—1 pint black beans, 2 quarts of cold water. Boil five hours. Add a ham bone or a few salt pork ribs, 1 onion, pepper, salt, 3 cloves, a pinch of mustard. Be sure there are two

9

quarts when done. When ready to serve, pour over the croutons, sprinkle on top the pulverized yolks of 2 hard-boiled eggs and a little lemon juice.—[Mrs. F. I. Storer.

LOBSTER SOUP WITH MILK.—Meat of a small lobster chopped fine, 3 crackers rolled fine, butter size of an egg, salt and pepper to taste, and a speck of cayenne. Mix all in the same pan and add gradually a pint of boiling milk, stirring all the time. Boil up once and serve.—[Miss Barry.

CLAM SOUP.—25 small clams, 1 quart of milk, half cup of butter, 3 potatoes, 2 large tablespoonfuls of flour, salt, pepper. The clams should be chopped fine and put in a colander to drain. Pare the potatoes and chop rather fine. Put them on to boil with the milk, in a double kettle. Rub the butter and flour together until perfectly creamy, and when the milk and potatoes have been boiling fifteen minutes, stir this in and cook eight minutes more. Add pepper and salt, and cook three minutes longer. Now add the clams. Cook one minute longer.—[Mrs. F. W. Kingman.

CLAM BISQUE.—1 quart milk, 1 pint clams and the water of the clams, 1 good-sized onion, sliced. Put these on in a double boiler, let stand 3-4 of an hour, stirring occasionally, then stir in for thickening 1 tablespoonful flour and 1-2 tablespoonful cornstarch in 1-2 cup cold milk. After ten or fifteen minutes, it is ready for serving. Pour into a dish in which are 2 well-beaten eggs, a piece of butter, salt and pepper to taste.—[Mrs. William H. Pierce.

CROUTONS FOR SOUP.—Cut stale bread in little squares and fry in drippings a golden brown. Put in soup tureen and pour hot soup over.—[Mrs. F. I. Storer.

PUREE OF CLAMS.—1 pint boiled clams. Chop hard parts fine. Cook 1 tablespoonful flour in 1 heaping tablespoonful hot butter,

The latest in Stationery always at Guyer's.

and add a little at a time 1 pint hot milk. Then add chopped clams, soft parts, salt and pepper. If the puree is too thick, add more milk or a little clam liquor. Remove from fire as soon as hot.—[Mrs. G. E. Tillson.

H. Y. C. CLAM CHOWDER.—1 potato for each person, 1-2 as many onions, medium size, 1-2 pound pork, 1 quart milk, 1 quart clams to 12 potatoes. Fry the pork, then add the onions, sliced, and fry, then sliced potatoes and small quantity of salt and pepper, cover with hot water, and boil until potatoes are nearly done. Separate the clams and chop the rims fine, add to the vegetables, and bring to a boil, then add clam water and milk and scald. Season to taste.

CLAM CHOWDER.—Separate 1 quart of clams, chop heads and straps, clean stomachs, and proceed as for fish chowder, using half clam juice and half water to boil the chowder, adding the milk when ready to serve, and seasoning after the milk is added.

FISH CHOWDER.—Cut some nice, fat salt pork into slices, fry a delicate brown, now put with the drippings into a kettle, adding in alternate layers sliced onions, potatoes, and nicely dressed fish, cut in square pieces, salt and pepper; cover with the water in which the bones and skin, also head of the fish have been previously boiled and strained out, to strengthen the chowder. Boil until vegetables are tender, then add boiling milk, and let it boil up once, and serve. If pork is not liked, add butter to season, when the milk is added.

SALT FISH CHOWDER.—Fry out 3 slices salt pork; fry 1 large onion in the fat; put in 1 quart sliced potatoes, cover with boiling water and cook. When done add 1 pint picked fish, freshened, and 1 quart hot milk; thicken with tablespoonful cornstarch.—[L. T. C.

Family Medicines at Guyer's Drug Store.

Copyright, Boston, 1898. **REVERE** by Cyrus Cobb, Sculptor.
"The Midnight Ride of Paul Revere," Alto Relievo Panel, in old ivory or bronze.
Actual size, 22 x 30 inches.

SPURR'S

Mocha **REVERE COFFEE.** Java

Trade-marks redeemable for Life of Paul Revere, 2 vols. and the
Paul Revere Panel.

BEST COFFEE IN THE WORLD.

Tested and endorsed by American Journal of Health. Send for
Paul Revere Letter, No. 8, containing 100 messages from consumers to
consumers regarding the satisfying quality of Revere Coffee.

HOWARD W. SPURR COFFEE CO.,
BOSTON, MASS.

13

Salt Fish Chowder.—Pick up small pieces of fish, soak in cold water until soft, pour off this water, add sufficient cold water to cover fish, put in half pint of tomatoes, let this come to a scald, then add to this 2 tablespoonfuls of flour and butter, evenly mixed with milk. After this comes to a boil, add 1 quart of hot milk. Put in tureen piece of butter before sending to table.

—[Mrs. W. J. Wyer.

Quahaug Stew.—1 quart quahaugs chopped very fine; boil 20 minutes, then add 3 pints of milk, thicken with butter size of an egg, 1 teaspoonful flour, 1-2 dozen oyster crackers rolled fine, mixed together. Do not let it boil after milk is added, or it will curdle. Serve with oyster crackers.—[Mrs. Julius Howland.

Fish Stew.—Cook 2 1-2 or 3 pounds of fresh cod or bass in sufficient boiling water to cover it, until nearly done. Add pepper, salt, butter, and a little thickening, also 1 quart of hot milk. Boil up once. Serve with oysters like oyster stew.—[L. T. C.

Clam Stew.—Separate 1 quart clams, chop heads and shoulders, boil 2 hours. Clean stomachs and add. Have 1 quart of rich milk scalding hot, add to the clams, which have been boiled in 1 pint each of clam juice and water. Season with salt, pepper, and butter.—[Mrs. F. I. Storer.

Corn Chowder.—6 ears of corn cut from the cob, 6 small potatoes cut in slices, 1 onion. Fry 3 slices of pork, then add the vegetables in alternate layers until all are used. Cover with boiling water, cook twenty minutes, stirring occasionally. Add 1 pint of milk, and let boil up once: salt and pepper to taste.

—[Mrs. C. E. Harris.

Fish Chowder.—5 pounds of codfish or haddock, 1-2 pound pork, 2 large onions, 1 quart of sliced potatoes, 1 quart of milk, 1 pint of water, 2 tablespoonfuls of flour, salt and pepper. Skin fish and cut all the flesh from the bones. Put bones in to cook in water; simmer gently ten minutes. Fry pork, cut in dice, then add onions, cut in slices. Cover and cook five minutes. Then add flour, cooking 8 minutes longer, stirring often. Strain on this the water in which the fish bones were cooked, and boil gently five minutes, then strain all on potatoes and fish. Season with salt and pepper, and simmer fifteen minutes. Add milk, and 6 Boston crackers, which have been split and soaked for three minutes in the milk. Let it boil up once, and serve.—[Miss Barry.

Guyer, the Druggist, Hyannis.

Fish.

"The silvery fish,
Grazing at large in meadows submarine,
Fresh from the wave, now cheer our festive board."

To Boil Fish.—The fish should be thoroughly cleaned, put in boiling, salted water, and kept boiling until done; if it stops before it is done the skin will break. In the absence of a fish kettle, it is best to boil the fish in a net; a new piece of mosquito netting, well washed, will do; it will greatly assist in its removal from the kettle and can be drained while in the net. If it be a kind of fish without decided flavor, it will be improved by adding to the water a small piece of onion, a bit of spice, or a dash of lemon juice. Serve with it drawn butter, with 1 or 2 hard-boiled eggs chopped fine and added the last thing.

Boiled Fish.—Any fresh fish weighing between 4 to 6 pounds should be first washed in cold water, then put into boiling water, enough to cover it, and containing 1 tablespoonful of salt, simmer gently thirty minutes, then take up. A fish kettle is a great convenience, and when you do not have one, keep a strong white cotton cloth in which pin the fish before putting into the boiling water; this will hold in shape. Hard boiling will break the fish, and of course there will be a great waste, and the fish will not look appetizing. There should be a gentle bubbling of the water, and nothing more all the time the fish is in it. A fish weighing more than 6 pounds should cook ten minutes longer for every additional 2 pounds. Boiled fish can be served with a great variety of sauces, which change the whole character of the fish.

—[Miss Barry.

Sauce for Boiled Fish.—1 pint of milk, 2 tablespoonfuls of

Bicycles and Sundries, Guyer Cycle Co., Hyannis.

flour, 2 of butter, salt and pepper to taste, 2 hard boiled eggs; mix the butter and flour together until smooth. When the milk boils stir 2 tablespoonfuls of it into the butter and flour, when well mixed stir into boiling milk slowly, then cook eight minutes, strain, then add the hard boiled eggs, which must be chopped very fine. Serve always with boiled fish. 2 tablespoonfuls of chopped parsley is a pleasant change from the hard boiled eggs.

—[Miss Barry.

BROILED FRESH MACKEREL.—Remove head and dark skin from inside, wash, and wipe dry. Butter bars of broiler and broil fish over bright fire, taking care not to burn. When done through, dip gridiron with fish on quickly into boiling water, remove fish to hot platter, and serve with a dressing made of 4 tablespoonfuls of melted butter, 2 tablespoonfuls lemon juice, a bit of chopped parsley, and a little pepper. Serve very hot, with either nice mealy baked or mashed potatoes.—[Mrs. F. I. Storer.

BAKED FISH.—Clean the fish thoroughly, wipe dry, salt inside. Stuff with any kind of dressing preferred and confine by passing coarse thread around it to hold it firmly. When ready lay it upon a buttered paper in baking pan, sprinkle with pepper and salt, then lay slices of sweet salt pork on top to season it. A good, steady heat should be kept up and the fish basted often until nearly done, then stop to allow the outside to become crisp and a delicate brown. If basted often the fish will be moist and delicious and done clear through.

BAKED FISH.—Clean and wipe fish, rub with salt, stuff and sew up. Cut gashes in sides of fish and put narrow strips of pork in each gash. Rub with butter, salt, and pepper. Dredge with flour. Bake in a hot oven one hour. Stuffing for fish: 1 cup cracker crumbs, 1-4 cup melted butter, 1 saltspoonful salt, 1 teaspoonful chopped onion, 1 teaspoonful chopped parsley, 1 teaspoonful chopped capers, 1 teaspoonful chopped pickles. Mix well.

—[Mrs. Lydia F. Crowell.

BAKED FISH.—A fish weighing about 5 pounds, 3 large or 5 small crackers, 1-4 of a pound of salt pork, 2 tablespoonfuls of salt, 1-4 of a teaspoonful pepper, 1-2 of a tablespoonful of chopped parsley, 2 tablespoonfuls of flour. Roll the crackers very fine, and add to them the parsley, 1 tablespoonful of chopped pork, 1-2 the pepper, 1-2 a tablespoonful of salt, and cold milk to moisten well. Put this into the body of the fish, and fasten with skewers. Cut gashes across fish about 1-2 inch deep, and 2 inches long, cut rest of pork in strips, and put these in the gashes. Put the fish into baking pan and dredge well with salt, pepper and flour, cover bottom of pan with water and put into a rather hot oven; bake one hour, basting often with gravy in pan, dredging each time with flour, salt and pepper. The water in the pan must be often renewed, as the bottom is only covered each time. Baste fish every fifteen minutes. When fish is cooked, lift carefully from pan, placing in centre of dish on which it is to be served. Make a brown gravy, garnish fish with slices of lemon and sprigs of parsley.—[Miss Barry.

BAKED HALIBUT STEAKS.—Trim the steaks, lay them in a roasting pan, and for 2 pounds use 1 cup cream, (or milk if necessary) 1 teaspoonful of flour, 1 tablespoonful of butter, 1 teaspoonful of salt, and 1 saltspoonful of pepper. Dredge the steaks with the flour, add the seasoning and dot with the butter. Pour over the cream and bake fifteen minutes in quick oven.—[P. C. P.

BAKED SEA TROUT.—Split fish, removing back-bone, lay the fish, skin on bottom of pan that is well buttered, cover with thin slices of salt pork and sliced onions, pepper and salt. Bake ac-

—2—

cording to size of fish. Just before taken from oven pour over the fish 1-2 cup of milk.—[Mrs. W. J. Wyer.

MACKEREL BAKED IN MILK.—Put a split mackerel in pan, season with pepper and salt, and nearly cover with milk. Bake three-quarters of an hour in a quick oven, or until done. After removing the fish, add a little water to the milk, and thicken for gravy. If a richer gravy is desired, add a scant half-teaspoonful of Worcestershire sauce and 1 teaspoonful tomato ketchup.—[M. P. C.

GERMAN STUFFED FISH.—1 small bluefish, 1 sea trout and 1 perch, cut into pieces of three or four inches each; take a small quantity of fish out of each end of the slice, put the pieces in a chopping dish, than add 2 of bread, 1 egg, pepper and salt to taste, 1 small onion, then chop very fine and fill the cavities you have made in the slices of fish. Put fish in a porcelain kettle, season with a little salt, slice half an onion over the fish, cover with water; let it cook very slowly for one hour, and do not stir the fish, as it will break it; shake the kettle to keep it from burning on.—[Mrs. L. Arenovski.

FINNAN HADDIE.—Cut the fish in several pieces, put into a stew-pan, cover with half sweet milk and half cold water, set on stove where it will not burn, let simmer until tender, then flake the fish, removing skin and bones, dress with dots of butter, pepper, and a very little of the milk in which it was boiled, set in oven long enough to melt the butter, and serve.

A DELICIOUS SUPPER DISH.—Have half a dozen white perch nicely cleaned, but left whole; any small sized firm fish will do. Slice a medium size carrot, a small onion, and cover with water, boil until tender, add the fish, with salt, and a teaspoonful of sugar; simmer until well done, but not broken; carefully remove the fish onto a deep platter, then with the beaten yolks of 4 eggs, thicken

the broth, heating but not boiling, lest it curdles, pour over the fish and serve hot or cold.

FRIED FISH.—Fry pork enough so fish can float. Wash fish and dry with cloth, then roll in meal mixed with salt and pepper, and fry to a brown in boiling fat. Serve hot.—[O. H. C.

DROPPED FISH BALLS.—1 pint bowlful of raw fish, 2 heaping bowlfuls of pared potatoes, (let them be under medium size), 2 eggs, butter the size of an egg and a little pepper. Put the potatoes into the boiler, and place the fish, which has been picked very fine and measured lightly in the bowl, on top of the potatoes, cover with boiling water and boil 1-2 hour. Drain off all the water and mash fish and potatoes together until fine and light, then add the butter and pepper, and egg, well beaten. Have a deep kettle of boiling fat, dip a tablespoon in it, and then take up a good spoonful of the mixture, keeping it in as good shape as possible; drop into the boiling fat and cook until brown, which should be in a few minutes. Do not crowd the balls, and be sure the fat is hot enough. The spoon should be dipped in the fat every time you take a spoonful of the mixture.—[Miss Barry.

FISH BALLS.—Flake very fine 1 cup of boiled salt fish or any kind of tender fish that has been boiled will do. Have ready 2 cups of mashed potatoes, mix the fish and potatoes thoroughly, then add 1 well beaten egg, 4 tablespoonfuls of cream, a bit of butter and dash of pepper, beat all well, roll in small balls, dip in beaten egg, dust with crumbs, fry a golden brown in hot pork fat; have the fat boiling and three minutes will cook them.

SAUCE FOR FISH BALLS.—2 teaspoonfuls dry mustard, 1 teaspoonful salt, 1 teaspoonful sugar, 1 teaspoonful flour, 1 teaspoonful soft butter, 2 tablespoonfuls vinegar. Mix in order given in a sauce pan, add 1-2 cup boiling water; stir over the fire till it is smooth.—[Mrs. George F. Crocker.

ESCALLOPED SALMON.—1 can salmon, remove bones, spread between layers of cracker crumbs, seasoned with pepper, salt, butter, as for escalloped oysters. Layer of cracker crumbs on top, moisten whole with milk, bake in hot oven about half hour.
—[Mabel L. Baker.

SALMON ON TOAST.—Heat a cupful of cream, (or milk thickened with flour, and butter added), to which has been added a dessert-spoonful of butter, and pinch of salt ; stir into can of salmon and pour over rounds of buttered toast.—[Miss Esther L. Baxter.

SALMON CROQUETTES.—1 can of salmon, half as much fine bread crumbs, the juice of 1 lemon, a little salt and pepper, 2 teaspoonfuls of cream ; mix all together, form into croquettes, roll in egg and cracker crumbs and fry.—[Mrs. Ruth Bennett.

SALMON CROQUETTES.—Stir 1 tablespoonful butter and 1 of flour together until smooth, over the fire ; add 2-3 cup of hot milk, (water will do), boil up once, add 1-2 teaspoonful salt, 1-4 as much pepper ; remove, stir in the yolks of 2 eggs ; cool, then stir in 1 cup chopped salmon. Make into small rolls or cones, roll in sifted cracker crumbs, then in beaten egg, again in crumbs, and fry brown in deep, boiling fat.—[Mrs. Parker.

CODFISH TOAST.—Flake and wash 2 teacupfuls salt codfish; place in a saucepan with 2 tablespoonfuls flour and same of butter, mix thoroughly, and add gradually 2 cupfuls boiling water. Have ready several slices of hot buttered toast, pour the fish over, and serve.—[Mrs. Lot Crocker.

EELS.—Take the small round eels, cut in finger lengths, score them, season with salt and pepper, drop in boiling pork fat, fry until done through and a crisp brown.

FRIED FROGS.—Wash and boil ten minutes in salted water, drain, when cool dip in crumbs, then egg, and again in crumbs, fry a delicate brown in hot butter; be sure they are quite done; serve hot, garnished with parsley and slices of lemon.

—[Mrs. F. I. Storer.

Remember the name, Guyer Cycle Co., Hyannis.

Shellfish.

OYSTER STEW.—1 quart oysters, 1 quart water, 1 quart milk, good sized piece butter, salt and pepper. Put the oysters in a stewpan with a little flour sprinkled over them, add butter, salt, and pepper. Put in quart of boiling water, let it come to a boil, then add milk and let it boil up and it is ready for the table.
—[Mrs. Osborn Crowell.

ESCALLOPED OYSTERS.—To a 3-pint dish take a quart of oysters and 1 pound of crackers. Roll the crackers fine, a layer of crackers, a layer of oysters, pepper, salt and butter, until the dish is nearly full, then soften with milk. Let it stand an hour and bake in a hot oven about an hour.—[Mrs. Osborn Crowell.

BROILED OYSTERS.—Drain the required number of large oysters on a napkin. Rub the wires of broiler with melted butter, arrange the oysters on the broiler, and broil over a quick fire until the edges curl, turning often to keep the juice from escaping. Lay the oysters on crisp, well-buttered toast, dressing with salt, pepper, and melted butter. Serve at once.—[Mrs. F. I. Storer.

OYSTER PIE.—1 quart oysters, season the oysters with mace, 1-2 glass of white wine, 1-2 cup of very fine cracker crumbs, a few pieces of butter. Put them into a pie dish lined with paste, and add 1-2 the liquor, fill dish quite full, and cover with a rich paste. Bake till the crust is nicely done.
—[Mrs. Sara T. Hammond.

CREAMED OYSTERS.—Drain, wash, then boil 1 quart oysters; drain again, this time saving the liquor drawn out by the heat. Measure the liquor, adding enough milk to make a pint. Have hot, ready to add to a mixture of 2 tablespoonfuls of butter, and

2 tablespoonfuls of flour—as for drawn butter—making a thick cream. To this add the oysters, seasoning with butter and pepper.

—[Mrs. John Frost.

QUAHAUG PIE.—Make a crust as for meat pie and line a deep pie plate. Remove 1 pint quahaugs from their water and chop fine. Place them in a plate and sprinkle over them finely rolled cracker crumbs, pepper and butter to taste. Over all put a crust.

—[Mrs. Franklin Crocker.

CREAMED LOBSTER.—1 tablespoonful butter, 1 tablespoonful flour, 1 teaspoonful salt, 1 teaspoonful mustard, 1 cup cream, a 2 1-2 pound lobster cut in small pieces. Heat the butter, add the flour, salt and mustard, stir till smooth ; add cream gradually till smooth and thick; add the lobster. Serve hot.

—[Mrs. C. E. Harris.

CREAMED OR CURRIED LOBSTER.—2 cupfuls of chopped, boiled lobster meat, 2 cupfuls of cream or milk, 2 tablespoonfuls of flour, 2 tablespoonfuls of butter, salt and pepper to taste. Melt the butter without browning, add the flour, stir until smooth, add cream or milk, and stir until it thickens. Take from the fire, add lobster meat, and season. Turn into the farina boiler and serve when hot. For curried lobster, add one teaspoonful curry powder to sauce given above.—[Mrs. Lot Crocker.

FRIED SCALLOPS.—Wash well, dip in cracker crumbs, then in beaten egg, again in crumbs, fry in hot butter, or butter and sweet lard mixed, season with salt and pepper. Cook well a delicate brown, garnish with cress or parsley.

ESCALLOPED CLAMS.—Separate 1 quart of clams, chop heads and shoulders, clean the stomachs, use alternate layers of clams and cracker crumbs, bits of butter, salt and pepper, moistening all with equal parts of clam juice and milk, having the top layer of crumbs. Bake in moderate oven about an hour.

—[Mrs. F. I. Storer.

Meats.

"In selecting beef choose that of a fine, smooth grain, of a bright red color and white fat. The sixth, seventh and eighth ribs are the choicest cuts for a roast. Have the bones removed and the meat rolled, but have the butcher send the bones for soup. The flesh of good veal is firm and dry, and the joints stiff. The flesh of good mutton or lamb is bright red, with the fat firm and white. If the meat of pork is young, the lean will break on being pinched; the fat will be white, soft and pulpy."

ROAST TURKEY.—Singe (if needful) and remove pin-feathers. Wash thoroughly inside and out, and rinse with cold water. Turn the skin back from the neck and cut neck off quite short, replace the skin and tie with soft white twine or cotton yarn. Fill the breast and body with dressing and sew up with the yarn. Fasten the wings behind the back with a long skewer, or tie with yarn. Also tie the legs together at the joints where the feet were cut off. Sprinkle with salt and rub butter all over the turkey, then dredge thickly with flour. Cover the bottom of pan with flour, place turkey in and set in the oven until the flour is browned, then pour in water enough to rather more than cover the bottom of pan. Baste about every twenty minutes, adding hot water and dredging with salt, pepper and flour at each basting. Slices of raw salt pork may be laid on turkey instead of rubbing with butter, if preferred. If cooked in a patent baker of course the basting is unnecessary. For the dressing, boil (all together) and chop, the liver, heart, gizzard, 3 medium sized potatoes and 1 onion. Add 6 rolled crackers, butter size of an egg, 1-2 to 3-4 pound of raw salt pork, chopped very fine, powdered sage, savory, salt and pepper to taste.—Mrs. N. A. Bradford.

CHICKEN STEW.—Clean and cut up the chicken, and cut up

KEVENEY & BEARSE,

Main Street,

→✷ MEAT ✦ MARKET ✷←

DEALERS IN PROVISIONS.

Constantly on hand Beef, Pork, Mutton, Lamb, Poultry, Tripe, Ham,
Sausage, Pigs Feet, Liver, Butter, Lard and Eggs.
Also Vegetables of all kinds in their season at lowest cash prices.

U. A. HULL,

→✷ WOOD AND COAL, ✷←

Grain and Hay Dealer,

SOUTH AND OCEAN STREETS,

Hyannis, =:= =:= Mass.

O. F. BACON,

Wholesale and Retail Dealer in

Beef, Pork, Mutton, Poultry,

HAM, VEAL, LAMB, ETC.,

HYANNIS.

Orders by Mail or Telephone Promptly Filled.

A RECIPE.

Recipe for making the home pleasant and comfortable: Have your furniture re-upholstered in new material in late and handsome designs; have your carpets taken up, cleaned and relaid, by a modern and the best method. Mattresses will wear much longer by being occasionally renovated.

L. J. CANNON,

HYANNIS, MASS.,

Upholstering, Cabinet Work & General Repairing

Carpets Taken Up. Cleaned by Machinery, and Relaid. Mattresses Renovated, Curtain Hanging, Picture Framing, Etc.

small bits of pork with it. Put in water to nearly cover it. Cook until about done, allowing twenty minutes for dumplings. Thicken gravy a little if needed. Serve vegetables cooked separate.

—[Mrs. C. C. Crocker.

FRICASSEED CHICKEN.—Take a chicken of about 4 pounds, fry out 2 slices of pork, cover with water and stew the chicken until tender. Gravy: Take 2 eggs and a medium sized piece of butter. Toast bread and lay the chicken on it and pour the gravy over it.—[Mrs. George H. Smith.

BROILED CHICKEN.—Take a chicken, split it down the back, and place it in a kettle of boiling hot water, cook it until tender, then place it in a roasting pan, dredge it with salt and flour, and cook until a nice brown. Baste it every few minutes with melted butter from the pan.—[Mrs. Sara T. Hammond.

COTTAGE CHEESE.—Boil 2 chickens until tender, take out all the bones and chop the meat fine, season it to taste with salt, pepper and butter, pour into it enough of the liquor to make it moist, put into any mould you wish, and when cold cut in slices.

—[Mrs. M. L. Bearse.

POTTED PIGEON.—Clean, then stuff the pigeons with a dressing made as for turkey. Sew them up and truss. Put them in a kettle with water enough to cover them, and boil one-half hour, then take up and drain them, roll in flour, and fry brown in pork fat. Thicken the liquor in which they were boiled with flour, pepper, salt, cloves, mace, and catsup. Put the pigeons in this gravy and simmer two hours. Serve in the gravy. Add 1-2 glass of claret if you choose.—[M. P. C.

A DELICIOUS STUFFING.—2 dozen oysters chopped very fine, mixed with 2 cups of bread crumbs or cracker crumbs, an ounce of melted butter, a tablespoonful chopped parsley, a little grated lemon peel, salt and black pepper, and a little cayenne, a table-spoonful chopped celery, moisten with a little oyster liquor, a little cream and the well beaten yolk of one egg.

—[Mrs. E. H. Davis.

Roast Beef.—Always wipe with a wet cloth. Dredge on all sides with flour, salt, and pepper, and have a little flour in the pan. When the flour in the pan is brown, add a pint of hot water and baste very often, dredging with salt and flour after each basting. Roast a piece of beef weighing 8 pounds 50 minutes, if to be rare, but if to be medium, roast one hour and a quarter, and ten minutes for each additional pound. The heat for roasting must be very great at first, to keep in the juices. After the meat is crusted over it is not so necessary to keep up so great a heat, but for rare meat the heat must of course be greater than for meat that is to be well done. Putting salt on fresh meat draws out the juices, but by using flour a paste is formed which keeps in all the juices and also enriches and browns the meat.—[Mrs. C. C. Howe.

Braised Beef.—Take 6 or 8 pounds of the round of beef. Put 6 slices of fat pork in the bottom of the braising pan, and as soon as it begins to fry add 2 onions, a carrot and a turnip, all cut fine. Cook these until they begin to brown, then draw them to one side of the pan and put in the beef, which has been well dredged with flour, salt and pepper. Brown on all sides, then add 1 quart of boiling water. Cover and cook slowly four hours, basting every twenty minutes. Take up meat, and finish gravy as for any roast; strain, pour around the beef and serve.—[Mrs. C. C. Howe.

Pot Roast of the Shoulder of Lamb.—Put the lamb in a large, deep spider with a tight-fitting cover; salt and pepper it; keep about a pint of water in the spider and let it cook slowly on top of stove until almost done, then let water all boil out and brown it on both sides, then take out the lamb and turn off all the fat. Put in about 1 pint of water in spider and let it boil up to get the browned juice off the bottom and thicken with cornstarch. This makes a nice brown gravy.—[Mrs. J. S. Nicholson.

Roast Ham.—Wash the ham very clean and put on with cold water to cover and simmer gently for four hours, if ham weighs 12 pounds. Remove the skin and put ham in baking pan, cover with bread crumbs and 3 tablespoonfuls of sugar. Let it cook two hours in a moderate oven. Make a brown gravy as for all roast meats.—[Mrs. C. C. Howe.

New Way to Cook Ham.—The ham is first thoroughly washed and dried, then coated with a paste composed of flour, spices, and water, placed in oven to bake for three hours, basting every twenty minutes. Remove from oven, remove skin, trim off burnt crust, skewer on slices of lemon, and dot whole with cloves, after which the ham is placed in a dry pan and allowed to bake for another hour. A fruit salad to serve with the ham is made of oranges, bananas, grapes, and preserved pineapple. The juices are drained off, blended, and spiced.—[Mrs. J. J. C.

Veal Birds.—Slices of veal from the loin, cut very thin; remove the bones, skin, and fat, and pound until 1-4 of an inch thick, trim into pieces 2 1-2 x 4 inches, chop the trimmings fine with 1 square inch of fat salt pork for each bird, add half as much fine cracker crumbs as you have meat, season highly with salt, pepper, lemon, cayenne, and onion, moisten with 1 egg and a little hot water, as for veal loaf. Spread the mixture on each slice nearly to the edge, roll up tightly, and tie or fasten with skewers. Dredge with salt, pepper, and flour, fry slowly in hot butter until a golden brown, but not dark or burned. Then half cover with cream and simmer fifteen or twenty minutes. Remove the strings and serve on toast; pour the cream over them, garnish with points of toast and lemon.—[Mrs. Sara T. Hammond.

Pressed Beef.—Boil a piece of beef until tender, slip out the bones, cool, chop fine, season with salt, pepper, a little onion juice, a dash of cayenne ; moisten with some of the stock, put into a deep dish, cover with weight. Slice carefully, garnish with parsley or curled celery.—[Miss Carrie Crowell.

SPICED BEEF.—4 to 6 pounds from the middle cut of the shin. Wash the meat and cut into several pieces, cover with boiling water. Skim carefully as it boils, then simmer until the meat falls to pieces and the liquor is reduced to half a pint. Remove meat and season the liquor with salt, pepper, and sage, add it to the meat and mix with a fork until the meat is all broken. Pack in a brickloaf pan. When cold, cut in thin slices.
—[Mrs. Henrietta E. Chase.

BEEFSTEAK.—If your beefsteak is too tough for broiling, chop in chopping bowl very fine, season with pepper and salt, make into patties, and broil or fry in a dry, hot spider.—[Mrs. R. Bennett.

BEEF AU GRATIN.—Have some good slices of underdone beef and lay them in a well-buttered rather deep dish, sprinkling each slice as you put it into the dish with a little onion juice, pepper, salt, and chopped parsley. Alternate layers of sliced beef with layers of sliced ripe tomatoes. Moisten well with stock, sprinkle breadcrumbs over the top, and sprinkle breadcrumbs with grated cheese. Set in a hot oven until thoroughly heated and browned.
—[Mrs. C. F. Sleeper.

VEAL LOAF.—3 pounds veal, 1-4 pound salt pork, chopped fine, 2 teaspoonfuls salt, 1-2 teaspoonful pepper, 2 teaspoonfuls sage, 2 eggs, 1 teacup of powdered crackers. Mix well together, put in a bread pan, bake one hour. Serve cold in slices.
—[Mrs. H. C. Bacon.

MEAT LOAF OR BALLS.—6 pounds beef or veal, chop and pound until like dough; 1 pound chopped suet, 3-1 quart bread crumbs soaked in 1 quart soup stock or milk, 2 eggs, 1 teaspoonful pepper, little ginger, 1-2 teaspoonful salt, little mace. Work all well together, make loaf, bake from one-half to one hour, baste often with stock or butter. Can be made into balls for soup, or to fry, or rolled in cabbage leaves that have been partly cooked, placed in an iron kettle with a little gravy and browned.

—[Mrs. C. A. Bursley.

BEEF ROLL.—Take 2 pounds of raw, tender beefsteak, chop it very fine, season with salt, pepper, and a little chopped onion ; add 3 rolled crackers, 2 tablespoonfuls melted butter, and 1 well-beaten egg. Make into roll and bake about one hour ; baste with butter and water before baking.—[Mrs. Edward L. Chase.

SHEPHERD'S PIE.—1 quart of any kind of cold meat, 8 large potatoes, 1 small onion, 1 cupful of boiling milk, salt, pepper, and nearly a pint of gravy or stock, thickened with 1 tablespoonful of flour. Season the meat, which has been cut into dice, and put in a deep earthen dish. Grate the onion into the gravy and pour over the meat. Pare, boil, and mash the potatoes, add the salt, pepper, and milk, and 2 tablespoonfuls of butter. Cover the meat with this and bake gently half an hour.—[Mrs. A. G. Guyer.

STEAK PIE.—Cut meat in small pieces and season and cover with water. Let cook until tender, then thicken with a little flour. Make a good biscuit crust and bake in oven. Any good, juicy meat will answer.—[Mrs. Simeon Eldridge.

BEEFSTEAK AND OYSTER PIE.—Take 3 pounds round steak and cut in thin slices. Mix 3 tablespoonfuls flour with pepper and salt, sprinkle over oysters, and roll them in beefsteak, then place them in deep pie dish and place a cup in centre. Cover with rich pastry, quite thick, and cook slowly one hour and a half.

—[Mrs. E. A. Baxter.

A NICE BREAKFAST DISH.—Chopped cold meat well seasoned, wet with gravy; then take cold rice made moist with milk and 1 egg, season with pepper and salt; place in a platter quite thick, set in oven to heat and brown or fry in cakes in a frying pan.

—[Mrs. Lizzie Johnson.

TO COOK COLD MEAT.—Chop fine, add salt, pepper, put in a dish, cover with chopped onion, then cover with hot, creamed, mashed potatoes. Bake forty-five minutes. Very nice.

—[Miss Carrie L. Crowell.

HAMBURG STEAK.—Chop a slice of pork with the steak, season, and brown quickly in a hot frying pan.

HAMBURG TOAST.—1 pound Hamburg steak, butter size of an egg, 1 cup milk, salt and pepper to suit. Put butter in spider, when hot put in steak, cook until done, add milk, salt, and pepper. Serve very hot on slices of nicely browned toast.

—[Mrs. E. S. Gibbs.

FRENCH HASH.—Chop very fine any kind of meat, put in stew-pan, season with butter, pepper, and salt, put in some water and allow it to cook well; just before it is done add some cream. Have some bread nicely toasted, place in a large dish, and put a spoonful of hash on each slice, pouring any gravy that may be left over it. This makes a nice breakfast dish.—[M. S. C.

MEAT HASH.—Chop rather fine any kind of cold meat; corned beef is, however, the best. To each pint add 1 1-2 pints of cold boiled potatoes chopped fine, 1 tablespoonful butter, 1 cupful of stock; or, if no stock is on hand, 2-3 of a cupful of hot water and a heaping tablespoonful of butter. Season with salt and pepper to taste. Put a little butter in the bottom of the frying pan and when very hot put in the mixture and stir over the fire for about eight minutes, being careful not to burn. Spread smoothly; cover

H. H. Baker & Son's Department Store,

HYANNIS, MASS.

For well cooked food

Have Good Cooking Utensils.

For a pleasing table

Have Pretty Dishes.

For the right things to appease the demands of hunger

Have the Right Things to Cook.

For all these wants

Go to H. H. Baker & Son's Department Store,

Hyannis. The Cooking Utensil, the Material to cook, and the
Dish to serve it in, all found at their DEPARTMENT STORE.

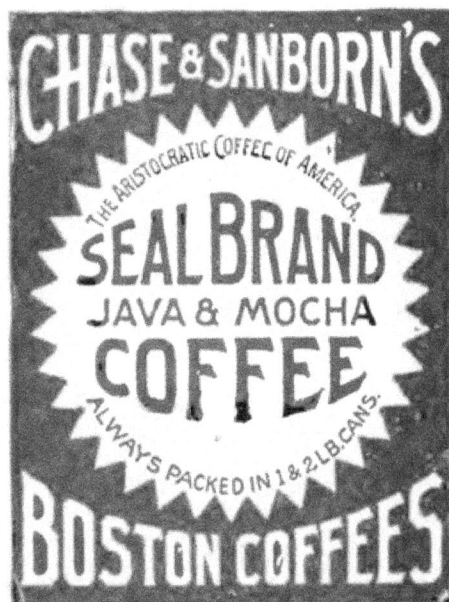

BE SURE AND GO TO THE STORE OF

S. B. MARCHANT,

HYANNIS, MASS.,

—: FOR THE :—

Best Groceries and Provisions.

We sell Nicholson's Electric Light Flour; call for trial package free. Also Fancy Plate Beef, Smoked Hams, Shoulders, Pork, Frankfort Sausages, Bologna, Pressed Ham, etc., Canned Goods, Teas and Coffees, Tobacco and Cigars, Confectionery. All kinds of fruit and vegetables in their season.

You will always find best goods and lowest prices at my store.

J. K. & B. SEARS & CO.,

...SOLE AGENTS FOR...

THE H. W. JOHNS'

PAINTS AND ROOFING.

These materials have an international reputation and the paints have proven to be peculiarly adapted to our atmosphere in the lasting quality of the different shades and their freedom from mildew and stain.

We claim for these paints superiority over lead and oil or any mixed paint on the market. Put up in packages from 1-2 pint to one gallon in all the different shades. Send for sample card.

the pan, set back where the hash will brown slowly. It will take about one-half hour. When done fold it like an omelet and turn onto a hot dish. Garnish with points of toast and parsley.

—[Miss Barry.

BAKED HASH.—Use 1 part meat, 2 parts potatoes, grate 1 onion, a little butter. Bake thirty minutes.

CREAMED DRIED BEEF.—For a family of six take 1-2 pound of beef, cover with cold water and gradually heat to boiling point. Drain and return to stove, stirring to dry off all the water. Add 2 tablespoonfuls butter and cook until brown, stirring all the time. Put in 2 teaspoonfuls flour, cook a minute, then add 2 cupfuls of milk, which will thicken quickly and form a creamy dressing. Dust with pepper before serving.—[Mrs. H. H. Baker.

CALF'S LIVER AND BACON.—Slice the liver, let stand a moment in boiling water, drain on napkin. Brown a few slices of sweet breakfast bacon, remove to a hot platter, drop the liver into the bacon fat, cook until tender but not hard, serve with the bacon and baked potatoes.—[Mrs. Storer.

DEVILED HAM.—Use pieces of cooked ham at least one-quarter fat; chop very fine. For a pint of this make a dressing of 1 tablespoonful sugar, 1 tablespoonful mustard, a little cayenne pepper, 1 teacup vinegar. Mix sugar, mustard, and pepper thoroughly and add vinegar gradually. Stir into ham and pack in small molds.—[Mrs. H. H. Baker.

Vegetables.

Now good digestion wait on appetite and health on both.
—*Shakespeare.*

"There is one thing upon which too great a stress cannot be laid: When the vegetable is cooked perfectly tender and ready to be removed from the fire, drain it thoroughly. Any amount of seasoning you may add will not give them the proper flavor if the water from the boiling is allowed to remain in them. Certain vegetables, like peas, string beans, spinach, brussels sprouts, should always be boiled uncovered. Be generous with good butter; it is the one great addition to a delicately cooked vegetable."—[E. P. T.

SCALLOPED CHEESE POTATOES.—Put in dish layer of sliced potatoes, add dots of butter, little salt, layer of grated cheese, then layer of potatoes; add milk to cover, and bake one hour. Serve when hot.—[Mrs. W. J. Wyer.

CREAMED POTATOES.—Heat 1 cup milk, stir in 1 heaping tablespoonful butter in which 1 tablespoonful flour has been mixed smoothly, stir until smooth and thick, add pepper and salt and 2 cups cold boiled potatoes sliced. Set over the fire until potatoes are thoroughly hot. Serve at once, as this is one of the dishes that is "spoiled by waiting."—[Mrs. E. S. G.

PREPARED CELERY.—Cut celery into inch pieces and boil in salted water until tender (one hour and a half sure). Make a sauce of 1-2 pint milk, 1 tablespoonful butter, a little pepper, and flour sufficient to make it the consistency of thick cream, pour over the celery and serve with roast beef.

—[Miss Carrie L. Crowell.

MACARONI AND TOMATO.—1 pint macaroni broken in inch pieces, 1 coffee cup of tomato strained, 1 tablespoonful chopped onion, 1 tablespoonful melted butter, 1 heaping tablespoonful of flour, 2-3 cup cracker crumbs, 1-3 cup melted butter. Boil macaroni twenty minutes, heat tomato, and fry the onion in the butter, stir flour in well and add to strained tomato, pour over macaroni, and put the cracker crumbs and butter mixed together well over the top and brown.—[Mrs. Sara T. Hammond.

MACARONI SAUCE.—Brown in a saucepan 1-4 pound veal with 1 cut-up onion, put into 1 quart of tomatoes with 5 cloves; season with salt and pepper, let simmer three hours, put through sieve. Boil macaroni half an hour in salted water, skim out and mix well with melted butter, pour over the tomato sauce, sifting grated cheese well through the whole.—[Mrs. C. A. Bursley.

BOILED RICE.—To boil rice so that all the grains will be separate and the mass perfectly dry, pick it over and take out any husks there may be in the rice; wash it in cold water and drain it, and then put it into plenty of boiling water salted. Boil it for twelve minutes; then drain it and cover it with the lid of the kettle or a thick towel. Let it stand ten or twelve minutes longer, until it is dry and the grains crack just a little. Then it will be ready to use.

RICE CROQUETTES.—To 2 cups of boiled rice put 1-2 of a well-beaten egg, the other half for the breadcrumbs. Roll in the breadcrumbs and boil in hot fat, the same as doughnuts.
—[Mrs. Simeon Eldridge.

CARROTS.—Wash and scrape them well. If large, cut them in two, three, or four pieces. Put them in boiling water, with a little salt in it. Full-grown carrots will require three hours boiling; smaller ones two hours, and young ones an hour. Try them with a fork, and when thoroughly tender take them up and dry them in a cloth. Divide them in pieces and split them, or cut them in slices. Season with butter, pepper, and salt. They should accompany boiled beef or mutton.—[Mrs. S. A. Hinckley.

BOILED PARSNIPS.—If young, scrape before cooking. If old, pare carefully, and if large, split. Put into boiling water, salted, and boil, if small and tender, from half to three-quarters of an hour; if full grown, more than an hour. When tender, drain and slice lengthwise, butter well, and put in oven to brown.
—[N. C. Hinckley.

SWEET PICKLE BEETS.—Slice 6 well-boiled beets, sprinkle over them 6 large spoonfuls of sugar, a little salt, a cup of hot water, 1-2 cup of vinegar, and a few pieces of cinnamon bark.
—[Mrs. Ruth Bennett.

CORN OYSTERS.—1 can corn, 1 cup flour, 1 teaspoonful baking powder, 2 tablespoonfuls milk, 1 egg, salt. Drop from spoon in hot lard and fry brown.—[Mrs. Irving Cook.

BAKED BEANS.—Parboil 1 quart of small white beans, throw off the water, slice 1 onion and place in bottom of pan or pot, add the beans, with a little salt, a tablespoonful of sugar if sweetening is desired, and a generous piece of butter; cover with rich milk. Bake several hours; watch carefully, and if more wetting is necessary, boiling water may be used.—[Mrs. James Otis.

CREAMED CABBAGE.—1 small cabbage cut in quarters and plunged into kettle of water boiling very fast. Add 1 scant salt-spoon of soda and a teaspoonful of salt. Boil with the cover off, and there will be no odor. Be sure that the water covers the cabbage all the time and boils very fast. Cook 25 minutes; remove the hard stems and pour over it a white sauce made with 1 cup milk, 1 tablespoonful each butter and flour.—[Mrs. C. E. Harris.

COLD SLAW.—Remove the outer green leaves from a firm head of white cabbage, cut the cabbage through the centre, cut out the tough stalk, put the cabbage into a large pan of salted cold water and let it stand for at least half an hour; then drain it, shave it on a cabbage-cutter, or chop it rather fine, and dress it with any of the salad dressings for which recipes are given.

—[Mrs. S. A. Hinckley.

DUTCHED LETTUCE.—Wash carefully 2 heads of lettuce, separate the leaves and tear each leaf in two or three pieces; cut 1-4 pound ham or bacon into dice, and fry until brown; while hot, add 2 tablespoonfuls of vinegar; beat 1 egg until light, add to it 2 tablespoonfuls of sour cream, then add it to the ham, stir over the fire one minute until it thickens, and pour, boiling hot, over the lettuce; mix carefully with a fork and serve immediately.

—[Jennie Kent Paine.

Salads and Dressings.

To make a perfect salad there should be a spendthrift for oil, a miser for vinegar, a wise man for salt, and a mad cap to stir the ingredients up and mix them well together.

—Spanish Proverb.

CHICKEN SALAD.—Boil, bone, and chop 1 chicken. Mix the meat with the same amount of chopped celery and salad dressing. Salad dressing without oil: 1 egg well beaten, then add 1 scant teaspoon salt, 1 scant teaspoon mustard, 1 large spoonful sugar, 1-3 cup vinegar added slowly, 1-2 cup milk or cream, 1 teaspoonful flour, small piece of butter. Cook in double boiler until thick and creamy.—[Mrs. H. C. Bacon.

LOBSTER SALAD.—1 can lobster (Bird Rock brand best); pour boiling water over lobster and let stand about five minutes; drain off this water, and repeat the same—this will take away the canned taste. Set away until very cold, then break (not cut) into small pieces, place in a salad dish, first a layer of lobster, then of quite finely cut celery, pour salad dressing over this, another layer of lobster, celery, and dressing, and so on, pouring dressing over last. For the salad dressing, use 2 tablespoonfuls hot butter, into which stir 1 large tablespoonful flour and add 1 cup milk, stirring to a smooth paste; mix 1 egg, 1 heaping teaspoonful mustard, 1 full teaspoon salt, 2 tablespoonfuls sugar, a pinch of red pepper, 1-3 cup of vinegar, stir into the hot milk or paste, and cook about five minutes or until the consistency of thick cream. This will keep several weeks in a cool place if placed in a covered glass jar.

—[Mrs. W. L. Case.

POTATO SALAD.—3 pints of cold boiled potatoes cut in cubes, 1 teaspoonful of grated onion, 2 tablespoonfuls chopped parsley; shake salt over all. Dressing for potatoes: Yolks of 2 raw eggs,

1-2 teaspoonful salt, 1-2 teaspoonful mustard, pinch of cayenne, 1 cup of oil, 1 teaspoonful vinegar, 1 teaspoonful lemon juice.

—[Mrs. E. H. Davis.

DUTCH SALAD.—4 quarts green tomatoes, 1 quart small onions, 1 quart small pickles, 1 head cauliflower, 1 bunch celery, 6 medium green peppers; chop all together and let stand twenty-four hours, covered with large cup of salt and water, then boil thirty minutes and drain very dry. Dressing : 6 teaspoonfuls mustard, 1 tablespoonful tumeric, 2 cups white sugar, 1 cup flour, mix with water to form a paste. Have 2 quarts vinegar to a boiling point, pour in the paste and stir until a thin custard.—[Miss E. H. Crowell.

OYSTER SALAD.—Half fill a salad bowl with white and finely cut lettuce leaves. On top of the lettuce place some oysters prepared in this way : Put the strained liquor from 2 dozen oysters into a saucepan, boil and skim it, add to it a tablespoonful of vinegar, with pepper and salt. Put the oysters in this to cook for three minutes; take them out, drain them, and set on ice to cool. Cover the oysters after they have been put on the lettuce with a layer of mayonnaise. Decorate the top with olives and capers.

—[Mrs. C. F. Sleeper.

GREEN PEA SALAD.—Have a pint of cold, cooked peas. Wash and drain a head of lettuce, pull leaves apart, and arrange in a salad bowl. Chop cold bits of lamb or fowl into small pieces, spread over the top of the lettuce, and then put the peas on top. Prepare a plain salad dressing with tarragon vinegar and serve, poured over the salad. A sprig of mint boiled with the peas improves this salad if cold lamb is used.—[Mrs. C. F. Sleeper.

CABBAGE SALAD.—1 small head cabbage chopped fine, 1 cup vinegar heated to very near boiling, beat 2 eggs, 2 tablespoonfuls sugar, 1 teaspoonful salt, 1 teaspoonful mustard together, pour into vinegar, stir until it thickens ; add 1-2 cup milk in which 2 tablespoonfuls flour have been stirred, stir all together, and add small piece of butter, pour over cabbage. Serve cold, garnished with parsley and small pieces of cold boiled beets.

—[Mrs. E. S. Gibbs.

CABBAGE SALAD.—Mix together about an hour before serving 1-2 white cabbage, 6 hard-boiled eggs, chopped quite fine. Make a dressing of 1 scant tablespoon mustard, 1 of sugar, 1-2 teaspoonful salt, pepper to taste, piece of butter size of an egg, melted. Mix dry ingredients, then add melted butter and 1-2 cup vinegar. Let all heat on the stove, then turn over the eggs and cabbage about an hour before using.—[Mrs. N. B. H. P.

BANANA SALAD.—Take 4 bananas and slice through the centre, juice of a large lemon poured over them; pour sugar over.

—[Mrs. John C. Bearse.

WALDORF SALAD.—Pare and cut into small blocks any kind of tart apples. Mix with them an equal quantity of celery. Dust with salt and pepper, sprinkle over a little lemon juice, mix with mayonnaise dressing, and serve on lettuce leaves.

—[Miss Florence B. Hinckley.

MAYONNAISE DRESSING.—1-2 pint olive oil, 1 teaspoonful mustard, 1-2 teaspoonful salt, 1-2 teaspoonful sugar, 1 tablespoonful lemon juice, 2 tablespoonfuls vinegar, yolks of 2 uncooked eggs, a grain of cayenne. Put the yolks of the eggs into a bowl with the dry ingredients, beat these until thick and light, add the oil a few drops at a time; when the mixture gets thick you can add a larger quantity of oil; when too thick add a few drops of vinegar; the last thing add lemon juice. The secret of success is in having everything cold.—[Mrs. E. F. Smith.

SALAD DRESSING.—1-2 cup vinegar, 1-2 cup cold water, 1 tablespoonful sugar, 1 teaspoonful salt and a little pepper, boiled to-

gether in a double boiler. When hot add 3 eggs, well beaten, 1 teaspoonful mustard, 2 teaspoonfuls flour.—[Mrs. E. E. Field.

PLAIN SALAD DRESSING.—Beat the yolks of 3 eggs, add a little salt, a sprinkling of cayenne, and half a saltspoonful of white pepper. Now beat in a few drops at a time, 5 or 6 tablespoonfuls of olive oil, and then just as gradually 3 teaspoonfuls of vinegar. If there is no celery in your salad, put half a teaspoonful of celery essence into the dressing. The mixture should be as thick as cold cream when ready for the salad. This is an excellent dressing.
—[Mrs. Lot Crocker.

SALAD DRESSING.—3-4 cup of milk, heat with 1 tablespoonful of butter, pour over yolk of 1 egg well beaten, added to a tablespoonful of flour moistened with a little cold milk, salt, sugar, pepper, and mustard to taste. Boil all together until it thickens, not too long, as it will curdle. Remove from fire and add 3 well-beaten whites of eggs and vinegar to taste. Use double boiler, and if one objects to oil think it will be liked.
—[Mrs. W. F. Ormsby.

SALAD DRESSING.—2 teaspoonfuls mustard, 6 teaspoonfuls sugar, 2 teaspoonfuls salt ; mix together until smooth, then add just hot water enough to make it creamy, beat in 1-2 cup melted butter and add the yolks of 6 eggs, 1 1-3 cups of milk, 1 cup of vinegar, lastly add the beaten whites of the 6 eggs. Cook in double boiler until it just comes to a boil, stirring constantly. This makes 1 quart of very thick dressing.—[Mrs. Osborn Crowell.

SALAD DRESSING.—1 egg, beaten, 1-2 teaspoonful mustard, 1-2 teaspoonful salt, 1-2 teaspoonful sugar, 1-4 teaspoonful pepper, 2 tablespoonfuls cream or butter, 1-2 cup vinegar. Set over boiling water to thicken.—[Mrs. Lydia F. Crowell.

CURRY SAUCE.—Chop 1 large onion fine, and cook in a table-spoonful of butter five minutes. Stir together 1 tablespoonful of curry powder and 2 of flour; add to onion and butter. Stir thoroughly and add 1 pint hot milk. Cook until smooth. Put in either fish, meat, or fowl as you prefer.—[Mrs. C. H. Allyn.

Luncheon and Chafing Dish.

SARDINES A LA PARKER.—Select 20 good-sized sardines, (imported), and remove their "jackets," using a knife with small, thin blade, lay them on tissue paper to remove the oil, taking care not to break the fish; then melt a tablespoonful of butter in the chafing dish and add thereto 1-2 gill sherry, the juice of half a lemon, and a dash or two of Worcestershire sauce; lay in the fish and cook about three minutes, turning them once. Serve on very thin slices of toasted brown bread.

CHAFING DISH OYSTERS A LA MARYLAND.—1 dozen oysters opened from the shell to the chafing dish, (this secures all the natural juice necessary) salt to season, a strong pinch of black pepper, a good generous dash of red or cayenne pepper, a teaspoonful of Worcestershire sauce, a generous lump of fine table butter, and a large wineglass (not less than 4 ounces) of good sherry wine. Light the spirit lamp, and when it is heated all through and simmers (boils) all over the dish, it is done. The oyster will be just plumped and the juice found to be fit for the gods. During the heating up to the boiling point they should be stirred occasionally with a silver spoon. This dish, carefully prepared, is no trouble whatever and when done far surpasses any other form of preparation that is open to the luscious bivalve.

—[Mrs. Sara T. Hammond.

OYSTER PAN ROAST.—Dozen large oysters, tablespoonful butter, half pint oyster juice, 2 slices toast, salt and pepper. Put butter in the chafing dish, as it creams add oysters and juice, seasoned with salt and pepper. Cover and cook two minutes. Serve on hot toast moistened with juice.—[Miss Mabel Penniman.

—4—

CURRIED OYSTERS.—Cook 1 pint oysters until plump, drain, reserve liquor, and strain through cheese cloth. Melt 3 tablespoonfuls butter, add half tablespoonful onion, and cook until yellow. Add 4 tablespoonfuls flour, mixed with 1 teaspoonful curry powder, 1-2 teaspoonful salt, 1-8 teaspoonful pepper. Pour on gradually oyster liquor and enough milk to make thick sauce. Add oysters, and soon as heated serve with toasted crackers.
—[E. E. Field.

OYSTER RAREBIT.—Parboil 1 cup oysters, drain liquor, melt 2 teaspoonfuls butter, add 1-2 pound cheese cut very fine, 1-4 teaspoonful salt, and a few grains of cayenne pepper; beat 2 eggs, add liquor, and add gradually to cheese, add oysters, and serve on toast.—[Miss E. H. Crowell.

WELCH RAREBIT.—Cut into small dice a pound of cheese; put into the chafing dish pan a piece of butter the size of a small egg. When it begins to melt put the cheese on it with a saltspoonful of salt, the same quantity of mixed mustard and cayenne pepper to taste. Stir with a heated spoon until the cheese begins to melt, then add 4 tablespoonfuls of beer or ale, then briskly and lightly beat, as much beer or ale again, and stir until it becomes a smooth, thick cream. Serve on hot buttered toast.—[Mrs. E. H. Davis.

WELSH RAREBIT.—Heat 1 cup milk to boiling pint, add 1 cup crumbed bread, 3-4 cup cheese. As soon as cheese is melted add 1 egg, well beaten, and salt to season. Serve on toasted crackers, hot.—[Mrs. George F. Crocker.

SHRIMP WIGGLE.—Melt 4 tablespoonfuls butter, and add 4 tablespoonfuls flour, mixed with 1-2 teaspoonful salt and 1-8 teaspoonful pepper. Pour on gradually enough milk to make sauce thicken. As soon as sauce thickens, add 2 cans shrimp, broken in pieces, and 1 cup canned peas, drained from their liquor and thoroughly rinsed.—[E. E. Field.

SHRIMP WRIGGLE.—1 can shrimps, 1 can French peas, 1-2 pint thick cream, 1 level tablespoonful flour, 1 tablespoonful butter. Put butter in first, then cream, then flour, and stir until smooth, then add the shrimps and peas. Cook about fifteen minutes in a double boiler, then put in chafing dish and cook five minutes, stirring all the time. Serve with hot rolls.—[Mrs. George F. Baker.

CHEESE FONDU.—Tablespoonful butter, cup of fresh milk, cup of fine bread crumbs, 2 cups of grated cheese, saltspoonful of dry mustard, 2 eggs, cayenne. Put butter in chafing dish: when melted, add milk, bread crumbs, cheese and mustard. Season with cayenne. Stir constantly and add just before serving, the 2 eggs, beaten light.—[Miss Mabel Penniman.

CREAMED TRIPE.—Parboil the tripe, cut into small pieces. Cook together over hot water a tablespoonful butter and a scant one of flour; add 1-2 pint milk and when the sauce is smooth put in the tripe. Cook three minutes, salt and pepper, and stir in slowly the beaten yolk of 1 egg, stirring constantly. Cook two minutes and serve.—[S. H. S.

ENGLISH TOAST.—Cut bread into square pieces and toast; take eggs out of shell, keeping yolks whole; beat the whites to a stiff froth, lay them around nicely on the toast, drop yolks in centre of white ring, and put in hot oven to bake a few minutes. When taken out of oven, pour little melted butter over toast.
—[Miss Carrie L. Crowell.

GOLDEN-ROD.—Boil 3 eggs thirty minutes, cut the whites in small pieces: make a white sauce with 1 cup milk, 1 heaping teaspoonful each of butter and flour; season with salt and a dash of pepper. Cook until thickened and stir into it the whites of the eggs, pour over 3 slices of toast; rub the yolks through a potato ricer and sprinkle over the top. Garnish with parsley.
—[Mrs. C. E. Harris.

52

CHEESE SOUFFLE.—White sauce of 1 tablespoonful butter, 1 of flour, 1-2 cup milk, salt; add 4 tablespoonfuls grated cheese; take from fire and add beaten yolks of 2 eggs, then stir in lightly the whites beaten stiff and bake in hot oven about twenty minutes.
—[Mrs. F. Thacher.

HAM RELISH.—1 cupful of cold boiled ham chopped fine, 1-2 cupful cream, 3 hard-boiled eggs, salt and pepper to taste. Scald the cream, rub the yolks of 2 eggs smooth with a little of the cream, add to the cream in the farina boiler with the ham. Press the whites of the 2 eggs through a sieve, add to the mixture; when thoroughly heated put on a heated dish, slice the remaining egg over the ham and serve.—[Mrs. Lot Crocker.

BREAD AND CHEESE OMELET.—Pour 1 cup boiling milk over cup bread crumbs; when latter has absorbed all the milk, season with salt and pepper and add 1-2 cup grated cheese with 4 beaten eggs. Fold and cook like ordinary omelet.—[Miss E. H. Crowell.

COTTAGE CHEESE.—Take 1 quart sour milk, set on back of stove until the whey is thoroughly separated from the curd; remove all whey by straining through cheese cloth. Add 1-2 teaspoonful of salt, piece of butter size of a walnut, 2 tablespoonfuls of cream. Form into shape.—[N. C. H.

Bicycle Lunches.

DEVILLED EGGS.—Take as many eggs as desired. Boil twenty minutes. Put immediately into cold water. When cold cut in halves and remove yolks. Rub the yolks smooth with pepper, salt, and mustard, a little melted butter and vinegar to taste, then press prepared yolks into the whites.—[Mrs. Geo. W. Doane.

EGG SANDWICH.—Boil eggs hard, discard the whites, mash the

yolks fine, add tomato catsup, Worcestershire sauce, salt, pepper, mustard, to taste. Spread between very thin slices of graham bread.

Egg Sandwich.—Boil eggs hard, separate the whites and yolks, chop whites very fine, press the yolks through a sieve and mix with mayonnaise or French dressing. Spread and cut rectangular.

Fig Sandwich.—Scrape out the soft portion of a dozen figs, rejecting the skins; rub this to a paste. Cut the thinnest slices possible from a loaf of either white or brown bread; butter and remove the crusts, spread over the paste, roll the bread carefully, pressing for a moment until there is no danger of the roll opening, then roll it in a piece of tissue paper, twisting the ends as you would an old-fashioned motto, or it may be tied with a piece of baby ribbon.

Chicken Sandwiches.—2 cups chicken chopped fine, 1 teaspoonful salt, 2 tablespoonfuls melted butter. Heat over the fire, and while heating mash the chicken to a paste. Cool and spread between very thin slices of bread, then cut in squares, triangles, or any fancy shape.—[Mrs. N. B. H. Parker.

Cheese Filling for Sandwiches.—1 cup grated cheese, 1 egg, 1 tablespoonful butter, 1 cup milk. Cook in double boiler until it thickens, set away to cool.—[G. B. H.

Russian Sandwiches.—Spread thin slices bread with slices of cream cheese or Neuchatel cheese, cover with chopped olives, mixed with a mayonnaise dressing. Cover and press together.
—[S. H. S.

Cheese Straws.—Sift 6 heaping tablespoonfuls flour on the pastry board, make hole in the centre and put into it 2 tablespoonfuls milk or cream, 3 tablespoonfuls dry grated cheese, 4 tablespoonfuls butter, 1-2 saltspoonful salt, dust of cayenne pepper, and yolks of 2 eggs. Mix all these ingredients to a smooth paste with the tips of the fingers, roll it out one-quarter of an inch thick, cut in narrow straws, and bake them light yellow on a buttered pan in a moderate oven. These straws make an excellent relish with plain salad.—[Miss Carrie L. Crowell.

Snow Balls.—3 eggs, 1 cup sugar, 4 tablespoonfuls milk, scant teaspoonful powder or cream of tartar and soda, pinch salt, flour to roll. Make in round balls, drop in hot lard; when done roll in white of an egg and sugar.—[M. B. Hallett.

Fruit Turnovers.—2 ounces preserved orange and lemon peel, 2 cups raisins, 1 ounce citron. Cook the orange and lemon until soft, scald the raisins, chop all together fine, moisten with syrup, teaspoonful lemon juice, tablespoonful brandy, mix thoroughly. Chop cup of lard and butter into cup of flour, mix 1-2 cup of cold water or more if needed, pinch salt if butter is fresh. Flour the board, roll out 1-2 inch thick, spread with butter, fold over, roll out again, spread with butter, roll out, cut in strips 7 inches long, 5 wide, put in spoonful of the fruit, fold over the sides, cut the ends in a point, fold over, baste over with milk or beaten egg, sift on little sugar. Bake from fifteen to twenty minutes, golden brown. Nice dessert.

Sardine Canapes.—Mix yolks of hard boiled eggs with equal quantity of sardines, rubbed to a paste. Season with lemon juice and spread on thin slices of bread. Cut in narrow strips.

Walnut Sandwich.—Chop English walnuts rather fine. Mix with mayonnaise dressing to make a soft paste. Butter thin slices of bread, spread with the walnut paste, press together and cut into any desired shape.

Olive Sandwich.—Mince cold chicken, tongue or lamb very fine and add equal quantity chopped olives. Mix with mayonnaise and spread.

T. CROCKER & SONS,

...DEALERS IN...

Ice, Coal, Wood and Groceries.

Wholesale Dealers and Packers of Fresh Fish.

Ship Shores and Ship Chandlery.

Railroad Wharf,   SOUTH HYANNIS, Mass.

BOOTS and SHOES

FOR MEN, LADIES AND CHILDREN.

Try The Knickerbocker Shoe,

For Ladies, Manufactured by

E. W. BURT & CO.

Warranted Hand-sewed, and Sold by

JAMES E. BAXTER, Hyannis.

CHEESE WAFERS.—1 tablespoonful butter to 2 tablespoonfuls of grated cheese; beat to a cream, put on crackers and brown in the oven.—[S. H. S.

POTTED MEATS.—An excellent substitute for the expensive potted meat fillings may be made from the odds and ends of cold meat minced and seasoned with Worcestershire sauce. Another appetizing sandwich is made from cold sausage crushed fine and spread on the buttered side of a biscuit. Boiled fresh cod or salmon made into a mince or paste used in combination with egg is always palatable. Thin slices of cucumber that have been upon the ice an hour or more are an addition to this filling. Good sandwiches can be made from all kinds of salads and their name is legion.

Sauces and Pickles.

Variety alone gives joy,
The sweetest meats the soonest cloy.
—*Prior.*

CRANBERRY SAUCE.—1 quart cranberries, 1 pint boiling water, 1 pint sugar. Wash berries in hot water and have saucepan or spider very hot. As soon as they begin to boil, cook just five minutes.—[Mrs. Teresa Crowell.

STRAWBERRY SAUCE.—Rub 1-2 cup butter and 1 cup sugar to a cream, add the beaten white of an egg and 1 cup of strawberries thoroughly mashed.—[Miss E. L. Baxter.

TOLMAN SWEET APPLES are very nice boiled in sufficient water to cover them and when cooked soft add sugar and cook awhile until syrup thickens. Flavor with extract of vanilla.
—[Mrs. H. H. Baker.

GINGER APPLE.—5 pounds sour apples chopped fine as for mince pies; equal parts apple and sugar; cut off outside of 3 lemons, using the juice to taste; 1-2 pound preserved ginger. Dissolve sugar, put in apples, lemon, and ginger, and cook until soft and clear.—[Mrs. Henrietta E. Chase.

GINGER PEARS.—1 peck hard pears sliced very thin, 5 pounds sugar, 6 lemons, peel 4 and slice very thin, slice other two without peeling; 1-2 pound preserved ginger. Put in kettle in layers and let it stand over night; in the morning put it on the stove and let it simmer five or six hours. Slice ginger.
—[Mrs. Elkanah Crowell.

RIPE TOMATO PRESERVE.—Ripe tomatoes skinned and broken, not cut, half as much sugar as tomato, 2 tablespoonfuls ground

ginger in 2 separate bags, 4 to 6 lemons, grated rind, white part cut off and lemon sliced. Put all together and cook quite thick.
—[Mrs. Henrietta E. Chase.

To Preserve Citron.—Cut into pieces 1 1-4 inches thick the round way of the citron, take out the seeds and pare, then put in some water and cook until soft, then take it out and drain and throw water away. Weigh the citron and put a scant pound of sugar to each pound of citron. Put in dish in layers and let it stand over night, or a day and night, until the sugar is dissolved, then put on the stove and let it cook until the syrup seems a little thick. If sliced lemons are used, put them in a little while before the citron is done ; if extract, after it is done. Seal in glass jars.
—[Mrs. Obed Baxter.

Sapson Apple Jelly.—Cover the apples with water and cook until soft, then strain through a cloth, taking nothing but the juice. Take not quite so much sugar as juice and place in a pan in the oven until heated through. Let the juice boil twenty minutes, then add the sugar and keep trying a little on ice until it hardens.
—[Mrs. Obed Baxter.

Preserved Barberries.—Put berries in kettle, cover with cold water and bring to the boiling point, then drain ; allow a pint of molasses to a pint of barberries ; boil the molasses, then put in the berries, and take off immediately.—[Mrs. Obed Baxter.

Rhubarb Jelly.—The following recipe for rhubarb jelly has been well tested : Wash the stalks thoroughly, cut into pieces one inch long, boil to a soft pulp, and strain through a jelly bag. To each pint of juice add 1 pound of loaf sugar and boil again, skimming often. When the juice "jellies" on the skimmer, remove it from the fire and pour into jars.—[Mrs. Obed Baxter.

Spiced Grapes.—7 pounds ripe grapes freed from the stems and washed, 5 pounds sugar, 3 teaspoonfuls each of cinnamon and allspice, 1-2 teaspoonful cloves, 1 pint of good vinegar. Squeeze the pulp from the skins and rub through a sieve to free it from the seeds. Cook the skins until tender in barely water enough to cover, then add the strained pulp, sugar, vinegar, and spices. Boil for one-half hour, or until thick and clear.

—[Mrs. Lot Crocker.

MUSTARD PICKLES.—1-2 peck onions, 3 heads cauliflower, 4 dozen large pickles cut up, 1-2 cup salt, 1-2 cup sugar, 1 gallon vinegar, 1-1 pound mustard, 1 cup cornstarch, 2 tablespoonfuls tumeric.—[Mrs. Geo. Smith.

CHILI SAUCE.—1 can of tomatoes, 1 large onion chopped fine, 2 cups vinegar, 1 tablespoonful salt, 1 cup brown sugar, 1-2 teaspoonful cayenne pepper, 1-2 teaspoonful clove, 1 teaspoonful ginger, 1 teaspoonful allspice, 1 teaspoonful cinnamon. Boil all together one and a half to two hours. Chop the tomatoes. Instead of canned tomatoes you may use 1 quart of ripe tomatoes, peeled by pouring boiling hot water on them.—[Mrs. Julius Howland.

SWEET PICKLES.—For apples, pears, peaches, quinces, stick a few cloves in the fruit, cook in a syrup of 3 pounds sugar, 1 pint vinegar, to 6 pounds fruit.—[Mrs. Wm. P. Lewis.

SLICED CUCUMBERS.—Slice thin 1 dozen cucumbers, leaving the rind on. Scatter salt over them and let them stand three hours, then turn off the liquor. Put to them 1-1 as many raw onions. Make a dressing of 1-1 teacup oil, the same of yellow mustard seed, 1-8 cup black mustard seed, 1-2 tablespoonful celery seed, and 1 pint vinegar. Mix this all together. No cooking.

—[Mrs. T. W. Nickerson.

PEAR CHIPS.—Pare and slice in small pieces 8 pounds of pears, 6 pounds sugar, 6 lemons, sliced, 1-1 pound preserved ginger. Mix and let it stand over night in preserving kettle. In the morning cook until tender.—[Mrs. E. H. Davis.

JELLIED PEACHES.—Provide first a dozen good sized peaches, and then half a box of gelatine, a cupful and a half of sugar, and a pint and a half of water. Soak the gelatine for two hours in half a cupful of water. At the end of that time put the sugar and the remaining water into a stewpan, and then let them boil for five minutes. Pare the peaches and cut them in halves, then cook them gently in the boiling syrup for ten minutes. On taking the stewpan from the fire turn the soaked gelatine into it; then set it in another basin containing cold water and stir occasionally until the mixture becomes cool. Before the jelly has had time to congeal, dip a mould into cold water and turn the mixture into it. Set in a cool place for three or four hours. At serving time dip the mould into warm water and turn the contents out on a flat dish. Serve with whipped cream or soft custard heaped upon the jelly. Many people will think the flavor improved by the addition of a tablespoonful of brandy of maraschino when the gelatine is put with the fruit.—[Mrs. Charlotte C. Bassett.

Bread.

It was a common saying among the Puritans: Brown bread and the gospel is good fare.

WHITE BREAD.—4 quarts bread flour, 1 teacupful sugar, 3 1-2 level tablespoonfuls salt, 1 yeast cake, 1 teacupful lard. Mix with 1-2 milk, 1-2 water to quite a stiff dough. Makes 4 loaves of bread.—[Mrs. Fred A. Hallett.

ROLLS.—Fill cup 2 1-2 times full of milk; white of 1 egg and 2 tablespoonfuls sugar beaten very light, then stirred into milk; small piece butter rolled into flour, 1-2 yeast cake; mould as other bread; mould down in morning, when raised light mould again, roll out and dip in butter and set to rise until light. This makes 34 rolls.—[Mrs. C. A. Bursley.

PARKER HOUSE ROLLS.—2 cups scalded milk, 3 tablespoonfuls butter, 2 tablespoonfuls sugar, 1 teaspoonful salt, 1 yeast cake dissolved in 1-4 cup lukewarm water, flour. Add butter, sugar, salt, to milk, and when lukewarm add dissolved yeast cake and 3 1-2 cups flour. Let rise until light, then add flour enough to knead, roll, brush over with melted butter, and shape. Place in pan one inch apart, let rise again, bake in hot oven fifteen minutes.—[Mrs. Irving Cook.

PARKER HOUSE ROLLS.—1 quart of cold boiled milk, 2 quarts flour, 1 large tablespoonful lard rubbed into the flour; make a hole in the middle of the flour, take 1 cupful yeast, 1-2 cup sugar, add the milk and pour into the flour with a little salt; let it stand as it is until morning, then knead it hard and let it rise, knead again at 4 in the afternoon, cut out ready to bake and let it rise again. Bake twenty minutes.—[Mrs. Dennis O'Neil.

HARTSON HALLETT,

Main Street, HYANNIS, Dealer in

Choice Family Groceries,

Grain and Flour, Dry Goods, Small Wares, and

......Paper Hanging......

ORDERS CALLED FOR AND PROMPTLY DELIVERED.

...M. B. ELDRIDGE...

DEALER IN

❖DRY AND FANCY GOODS❖

Small Wares, Germantown and Saxony Yarns.

Headquarters for Low Prices in Gloves, Hosiery, Corsets, Etc., Etc.

LADIES' AND GENT'S FURNISHING GOODS.

NEXT DOOR EAST OF DEPOT,   -   -   HYANNIS, MASS.

BROWN BREAD.—It is made of Franklin Mills flour, to be had at any of the grocers in town, in 6 1-8 pound packages: 5 cups flour, 1 cup molasses, 1 pint milk, if milk is sweet 1 teaspoonful soda, if sour 2 teaspoonfuls soda, pinch salt. Steam three hours in Royal baking powder 1-lb. cans about two-thirds full, and cover.

—[Mrs. E. M. Sprague.

BROWN BREAD.—1 cup rye meal, 1 cup graham, 1 cup Indian, 1-2 cup molasses, 1-4 cup flour, 1 teaspoonful soda, 1 pint sour milk, 1 teaspoonful salt, 1 tablespoonful melted butter.

—[Miss Susie Smith.

PRUNE BREAD.—1 quart whole wheat flour, 1 pint graham flour, 1 heaping coffee cup chopped prunes, even teaspoonful salt, tablespoonful sugar. Wash prunes and soak a few minutes; they should be of prime quality and soft; chop fine. Put all materials together; dissolve a Fleischman's compressed yeast cake in a little warm milk, add enough warm milk to make a soft dough. Let rise, when light stir briskly and pour into pan; let rise again, and bake in moderate oven.—[Mrs. James Otis.

CORN BREAD.—1 tablespoonful sugar, 1 tablespoonful melted butter, and 1 egg beaten together; add 1 heaping cup flour with 1 heaping teaspoonful baking powder and 1 heaping cup bolted meal. Mix quite soft with part milk and part water and bake in a hot oven.—[Mrs. W. G. Davis.

MUFFINS.—3 cups sifted flour, 1 egg, 1 teaspoonful cream of tartar, 1-2 teaspoonful saleratus, tablespoonful sugar, a little salt. Stir up with milk and water the thickness of plain cake.

—[Mrs. H. K. Hallett.

BREAKFAST GEMS.—1 egg, 2 cups flour, 2 tablespoonfuls sugar, 1 teaspoonful baking powder, 2 cups milk. Bake twenty minutes.

—[Mrs. Lizzie C. Johnson.

GEMS.—2 cups flour, pinch of salt, 1 egg, tablespoonful sugar, 2 teaspoonfuls powder. Stir up with milk about as for cake. Bake in hot gem pans.—[Mrs. M. B. Hallett.

GRAHAM GEMS.—1 1-2 cups sour milk, 1 teaspoonful soda, 1-2 teaspoonful salt, 2 tablespoonfuls molasses, 1-2 cup white flour, enough graham flour to make a stiff batter. They are not so good with sweet milk.—[Mrs. Lot Crocker.

RICE GEMS.—Take 1 cup boiled rice and moisten with 1 cup of milk, 1 well-beaten egg, 1 great spoonful sugar, a little salt, 2 cups flour in which has been added 2 teaspoonfuls baking powder. Sift flour and powder into the mixture the last thing. Have gem pans hot and oven the right temperature.—[Mrs. S. Eldridge.

SPIDER CORN CAKE.—3-4 cup corn meal, flour to fill the cup, 1 tablespoonful sugar, 1-2 teaspoonful salt, scant 1-2 teaspoonful soda, 1 egg, 1 cup sweet milk, 1-2 cup sour milk, 1 tablespoonful butter. Mix the meal, flour, sugar, salt and soda, beat the egg, add the sour milk and one-half the sweet milk, stir this into the dry mixture, melt the butter in a hot spider or shallow round pan and pour the mixture into it; pour the other half cup of sweet milk over the top, but do not stir it in. Bake twenty minutes in a hot oven.—[Mrs. E. H. Davis.

APPLE JOHNNY CAKE, (without eggs).—1 pint white meal, 2 tablespoonfuls sugar, salt, 1-2 teaspoonful soda, 1 teaspoonful cream of tartar, milk enough to mix quite soft, add 3 apples pared and sliced.—[Mrs. George F. Crocker.

BREAKFAST WAFERS.—1 pint flour, 1 teaspoonful baking powder, 1-2 teaspoonful salt, 3 eggs, 1 1-4 cups milk, 1 tablespoonful melted butter. Mix in order given, add beaten yolks of eggs with milk, then melted butter, and whites last, well beaten.
—[Mrs. George F. Crocker.

TEA GEMS.—2 cups flour, 2 teaspoonfuls Royal baking powder, 2 tablespoonfuls sugar, a little salt, 2 eggs. Mix with milk and beat well; have it so you can drop from a spoon into your hot gem pan. Bake twenty minutes.—[Mrs. C. B. Marchant.

TEA CAKES.—2 1-2 cups flour, 1-2 teaspoonful soda, 1 teaspoonful cream of tartar, 1-2 cup sugar, 1-2 teaspoonful salt, 1 egg, 1 cup milk, tablespoonful melted butter. Mix in order given, bake in gem pans. Add 1 cup of berries and it makes delicious berry cake.—[Mrs. George F. Crocker.

Cake.

Would ye both eat your cake and have your cake?
—*Heywood.*

ANGELS' FOOD.—The secret in making angels' food lies in the baking of it. Sift 1 cup flour and 1 teaspoonful cream of tartar several times through a fine sieve. Beat the whites of 9 eggs to a stiff froth and to them add 1 1-2 cups sifted granulated sugar; mix carefully into this, stirring constantly, the sifted flour and add 1 teaspoonful extract of vanilla. Pour this batter into an ungreased pan and bake in a slow oven for forty-five minutes. When baked, turn the pan upside down on something that will admit of the air passing under it, and allow it to stand until the cake falls from the tin. Ice with white icing. Be careful in making this cake to have all the ingredients as light as possible.

—[Mrs. Eleazer Baker.

MOCK ANGEL CAKE.—1 cup sugar, 1-2 cup butter creamed together, 1-2 cup milk, 1 cup flour, 1-2 cup cornstarch, 1-2 teaspoonful baking powder, the whites of 4 well-beaten eggs, 1 teaspoonful vanilla. Frosting: 1-2 square chocolate, 1 cup confectionery sugar, butter size of a nutmeg; melt together, then moisten with milk, flavor with vanilla.—[Mrs. Hattie A. Hopkins.

PLAIN CAKE.—Mix well together 1 cup sugar, 1-2 cup butter; add 2 eggs, and mix well, 1-2 cup milk, 1 even teaspoonful Royal baking powder, sift with the flour; I never measure flour, use your own judgment; vanilla or lemon. Have your oven the right heat, as there is as much in baking as making. Beat until your arm aches. Use hands for mixing sugar and butter.

—[Mrs. Emeline Bearse.

PLAIN CAKE.—2 eggs, 2 cups sugar, 2-3 cup butter, 3 cups sift-

H. B. CHASE & SONS,

(Established 1818)

GRAIN, HAY AND COAL.

STORE OPPOSITE DEPOT.

EDWARD L. CHASE.

EDWARD L. CHASE,

CONVEYANCER,

NOTARY PUBLIC,

JUSTICE OF THE PEACE.

FIRE, MARINE AND LIFE INSURANCE.

IYANOUGH HOUSE, HYANNIS, MASS.

T. H. SOULE, Jr., Prop'r.
FIRST-CLASS LIVERY STABLE CONNECTED.

ed flour, 1 teaspoonful cream of tartar, 1-2 teaspoonful of saleratus. Stir up with milk. Lemon or vanilla to flavor.

—[Mrs. H. K. Hallett.

LIGHTNING CAKE.—1 cup sugar, into that sift 1 1-4 cups flour and 1 scant teaspoonful yeast powder; melt 1-2 cup butter and break 2 eggs into it, then fill the cup with milk, turn this into the flour and sugar, mix well and flavor.—[Mrs. W. P. Saint.

ONE EGG CAKE.—1 cup sugar, 1 egg, 2-3 cup milk, 1-2 cup butter, 1 teaspoonful cream of tartar, 1-2 teaspoonful saleratus, salt, 1 teaspoonful extract, 1 1-2 good cups flour.

—[Mrs. Esther A. Baker.

CAKE WITHOUT CREAM TARTAR.—Cream 1 cup butter and 2 cups sugar together, then add 1 cup of milk and 3 eggs. Stir all together. Lastly 3 cups pastry flour and a piece of soda about as large as a pea. Very nice and will keep any length of time. Flavor with whatever you choose.—[Mrs. Simeon Eldridge.

ORIGINAL NUT CAKE.—Cream 1 small cup sugar and small 1-2 cup butter, add small 1-2 cup milk, 1 teaspoonful vanilla and 3 drops almond, 1 1-4 cups flour and the beaten whites of 2 large or 3 small eggs, 1 teaspoonful baking powder. After beating until very smooth and fine, spread in shallow pan and cover the top with a small cup of walnut meats chopped fine; bake in slow oven. It is best to try a little to make sure that the nuts do not sink into the cake; in case they do, a little more flour is needed.

—[Mrs. C. W. Megathlin.

DELICATE SPICE CAKE.—Rub 2-3 cup of butter and 2-3 cup of sugar together, then add 3 well-beaten eggs and 2-3 cup molasses, and stir well; then 2 1-2 generous cups flour, 2 teaspoonfuls baking powder, 1 tablespoonful mixed spices, a little salt, and lastly 1 cup milk. Bake slowly in a shallow pan. Fruit may be added if desired.—[Mrs. E. C. Baker.

RIBBON CAKE.—1 1-2 cups sugar, 1-2 cup butter, 3 eggs, 1-2 cup milk, 2 cups flour, 1 teaspoonful cream of tartar, 1-2 teaspoonful saleratus. Take out 1 cup of the above mixture and add to it 2 tablespoonfuls molasses, 1 teaspoonful cinnamon, 1 teaspoonful clove, 1-2 cup of raisins well floured. Bake in three layers with fruit in the middle.--[Mrs. Obed Baxter.

HARLEQUIN CAKE.—1 cup sugar, 1-2 cup butter, 1-2 cup milk, 2 full cups flour (after sifting several times), 1 heaped teaspoonful baking powder sifted in the flour, little salt and flavor; now add the whites of 4 eggs beaten to a stiff froth, beat this several minutes, and divide into three parts, reserving the largest part for the white; to one part add a small square of melted chocolate, to the other add a few drops of pink or other color. Drop in cake pan large spoonfuls of the white, and on this first a small spoonful of chocolate, then of pink, then of white, and so on. If baked in a moderate oven about thirty minutes it should be fine and light. Frost with white or chocolate. A very pretty cake cut in squares.
—[Mrs. W. L. Case.

SUNSHINE CAKE.—Whites of 7 small eggs, yolks of 5, 1 cup granulated sugar, 3-4 cup flour, 1-3 teaspoonful cream of tartar and a pinch of salt added to whites before whipping. Sift, measure, and set aside flour and sugar; separate the eggs, putting whites in mixing bowl and yolks in small bowl; beat yolks to a very stiff froth; whip whites about one-half, add cream of tartar, whip until very stiff; add sugar to whites and beat in, then yolks and beat in, then flavor and beat in, then flour and fold lightly through. Bake at once 20 to 40 minutes.—[Mrs. H. H. Baker.

PORK CAKE.—1 cup salt pork chopped very fine, add 1 cup boiling water, 1 cup molasses, 1 cup sugar, 1 teaspoonful soda, 1 teaspoonful cinnamon, 1-2 teaspoonful clove, 2 cups raisins, 1 cup currants, 3 cups flour. This makes 2 loaves.
—[Miss Esther H. Coffin.

WHITE SPONGE CAKE.—Whites of 5 eggs, 1 cup flour, 1 cup sugar, 1 teaspoonful baking powder, flavor with vanilla. Bake in quick oven.—[Mrs. W. F. Ormsby.

CORNSTARCH CAKE.—1 cupful each butter and sweet milk, 1-2 cup cornstarch, 2 cupfuls each sugar and flour, whites of 5 eggs beaten to a stiff froth, 2 teaspoonfuls cream of tartar, 1 of soda, flavor to taste. Bake in gem tins.—[Miss Hattie Ormsby.

RAISE CAKE.—1 quart flour, (sifted), 2 1-2 cups sugar, teaspoonful cinnamon, half one of cloves and allspice. Mix all together dry, then add 1 cup thick sour cream, (any shortening can be used), 1-2 cup molasses, teaspoonful soda, salt, and sour milk to make about as stiff as pound cake. This makes three small loaves.—[Mrs. F. Thacher.

CHOCOLATE CAKE.—Cream 1 cup sugar and a small half cup of butter, add 1-2 cup milk, 1 teaspoonful vanilla and 5 drops lemon, 1 cup flour, (measure before sifting) and sift three or four times with a teaspoonful baking powder, the whites of 4 eggs beaten stiff. Put flour, powder, and eggs in together and stir until very smooth, bake in shallow pan or Washington pie tins. Chocolate filling or frosting: 1 1-2 cups sugar, 1-2 cup water; boil until it will drop from a spoon thick but not quite string; take from fire, add 2-3 cup Baker's chocolate, stir until smooth, add teaspoonful vanilla and the beaten yolks of 3 eggs, beat again and spread. This should be a smooth, soft mixture that will spread and glaze, but not grain or run.—[Mrs. C. W. Megathlin.

ORANGE CAKE.—2 cups sugar, 1-2 cup water, 2 cups flour, 5 eggs, leaving out the whites of 2, juice and rind of 1 orange, 1 teaspoonful cream of tartar, 1-2 teaspoonful soda; beat the yolks stiff, add sugar, then the whites of the eggs after beating to a stiff froth, then water with soda, the orange and flour with cream of tartar. Bake in two good-sized pans, slice oranges and put in between. Frosting : Whites of 2 eggs, 2 cups sugar, juice and rind of 1 orange.—[Mrs. E. F. Smith.

ORANGE CREAM CAKE.—1 cup sugar, 1-2 cup butter, the yolk of 1 and whites of 2 eggs, 1-2 cup milk, 1 1-2 cups flour and 1 heaping teaspoonful baking powder. Cream : 1-2 cup boiling water, 1 tablespoonful cornstarch, 1 cup sugar, juice and rind of 1 large or 2 small oranges, and yolk of 1 egg. When cool spread between the three layers.—[Mrs. Abna L. Bearse.

WHITE CAKE.—2 cups sugar, 1 cup butter, whites 6 eggs, 1-2 cup milk, 3 cups flour, 1 teaspoonful baking powder. Flavor with almond. Ice thickly with white icing.—[Miss Mabel L. Baker.

WHITE FRUIT CAKE.—1 cup of butter beaten to a cream, add 2 cups of sugar, 3 cups of flour in which 2 teaspoonfuls of cream tartar and 1 of soda have been sifted, and the stiffly beaten whites of 6 eggs. Bake in jelly cake tins, and when done, but still hot, put between the layers the following filling : Chop fine 1-4 pound each of figs, seeded raisins, citron, preserved ginger and blanched almonds, and stir them into whites of 3 eggs beaten stiff, a teacup of powdered sugar, and the juice of 1 lemon. Put this between the layers, and frost the whole thickly with the white of 1 egg beaten with the juice of 1-2 lemon, and 1 cup of powdered sugar.—[Mrs. Albert Bacon.

WEDDING CAKE.—1 pound flour, 1 pound butter, 1 pound sugar, 2 pounds currants, 2 pounds raisins, 1 pound citron, 1 cup molasses, 9 eggs, 4 tablespoonfuls brandy, 1 teaspoonful soda, cloves, cinnamon, and nutmeg to taste. Makes 3 loaves.

—[Mrs. Wm. C. Baker.

LILY CAKE.—1-2 cup butter, 1 cup sugar, 1-2 cup milk, 1 3-4 cups flour, 2 1-2 teaspoonfuls powder, whites of 3 eggs, 1-2 teaspoonful lemon, 2-3 teaspoonful vanilla. Cover with chocolate frosting.—[Mrs. M. Bacon.

DUTCH APPLE CAKE.—1 pint flour, 1-2 teaspoonful salt, 1-2 teaspoonful soda, 1 teaspoonful cream tartar, 1-4 cup butter, 1 egg, scant cup milk, 4 sour apples, 2 tablespoonfuls sugar. Mix dry ingredients in order given, rub in butter. Beat egg, mix with milk, then stir all together. Slice apples, place on top, and put on sugar; to be eaten with sauce.—[Mrs. George F. Crocker.

CREAM CAKES.—Shells: Boil 1-2 cup butter and 1 cup hot water, stir in 1 cup sifted flour; cool, then add 3 eggs. Bake in drops. Cream: 2 cups milk scalded, stir in until thick 3 eggs, 2-3 cup sugar, 2 teaspoonfuls wet cornstarch; mix together; flavor.—[Mrs. Imogen Crocker.

MARSHMALLOW FILLING.—3-4 cup sugar, 1-4 cup milk, 1-4 pound marshmallow, 2 tablespoonfuls hot water, a little vanilla extract. Heat sugar and milk to nearly boiling; do not stir; melt the marshmallow by breaking up and adding the hot water. Cook until smooth, then add the hot milk and sugar slowly, and beat. Remove, and stir until cool, then add vanilla and fill. Good for frosting if desired.—[Miss Carrie L. Crowell.

COFFEE FROSTING.—1 cup coffee boiled with a cup of sugar, drop a little into water, if it hardens pour it slowly on the well beaten whites of 2 eggs; when cold put between cakes and on top.—[Miss Carrie L. Crowell.

FRUIT FILLING.—White of 1 egg well beaten, 1 cup of powdered sugar, 1 cup of any kind of fruit, such as grated apple, pear, etc.—[Mrs. John C. Bearse.

CARAMEL FILLING.—1 cup sugar, 3-4 cup milk, butter size of an egg. Boil fifteen minutes, stir while boiling, until right quantity to spread between cakes.—[Mrs. John C. Bearse.

RAISIN FILLING FOR CAKE.—Boil 1 cup sugar and 4 tablespoonfuls of water until it threads from a fork. Pour the hot syrup over white of one egg beaten stiff, stirring all the time. Add 1 cup chopped raisins, or 1-2 cup chopped raisins and 1-2 cup chopped nuts.—[Mrs. G. E. Tillson.

NUT CAKES.—1 cup brown sugar, 1 cup English walnut meats slightly broken, not chopped, 3 heaping tablespoonfuls flour, 1-4 teaspoonful baking powder, 1-3 teaspoonful salt, 2 eggs. Beat the eggs, add the sugar and salt, flour and powder, and lastly meats. Drop in buttered tins. Bake until brown. Remove from tins immediately after baking.—[M. S. C.

SOFT GINGERBREAD.—1-2 cup molasses, 1-2 cup sugar, 1-2 cup hot water, 3 cups flour, large tablespoonful butter, teaspoonful ginger, teaspoonful soda, little salt.—[Mrs. K. R. Bearse.

SPICED SNAPS.—1 pint flour, 1 teaspoonful each of cinnamon and ginger, 1-2 teaspoonful of nutmeg, 1 cup molasses, 1-2 cup brown sugar, 1 teaspoonful soda, 1-2 cup butter. Heat the molasses and sugar together till sugar is melted. Dissolve the soda in a little warm water and stir quickly into molasses, add the butter, then the flour mixed with the spices. Add enough more flour to roll thin. Cut out and bake in a quick oven.

—[Miss Esther L. Baxter.

GINGER SNAPS.—1 coffee cup New Orleans molasses, 1 cup butter, 1 cup sugar. Place them on the stove and let it come to a boil, then take off immediately and add a teaspoonful of soda, a tablespoonful of ginger and 1 egg. Roll thin and bake quickly.

—[Mrs. W. A. Baldwin.

GINGER SNAPS.—1 cup molasses, 1-4 cup sugar. Boil together fifteen minutes. While boiling stir in 1-2 cup butter or lard, 1 tablespoonful ginger. When cool add 1 teaspoonful soda, and flour enough to roll. Roll very thin and bake quickly.

—[Mrs. Daniel Bearse.

CHAS. E. HARRIS, M. D.,

HYANNIS, MASS.

Office at HALLETT HOUSE, Hyannis Port, Daily.   Telephone
Connection.

ALFRED C. DREW,
ELECTRICIAN

Electric Bells. Battery Materials, Electric Supplies.

General Repair Work.

Bicycle Repairs, Lathe Work & Brazing, Bicycle Sundries, Fittings, &c.

HYANNIS, - - - - MASS.

S. A. PUTNAM,
PHOTOGRAPHER

HYANNIS, MASS.

Portraits and Landscapes, Crayon, Pastel, and Water Color Portraits
made to order.   Please call and examine specimens.
Frames and Fittings on hand or furnished at short notice.

DEVELOPING AND PRINTING FOR AMATEURS.

JOHN H. SMITH,
MARKET GARDENER

Ice, Milk, Etc.,

HYANNIS PORT, - - MASS.

GINGER CAKES.—1 cup of shortening, 1 cup of sugar, 1 of molasses, 1 of milk, 1 teaspoonful of saleratus, 1 tablespoonful of ginger, flour enough to roll out.—[Mrs. J. R. Hall.

FRUIT COOKIES.—1 1-2 cupfuls of sugar and 1 of butter, worked to a cream; add 3 eggs well beaten, 1-2 cupful molasses, 1 teaspoonful soda dissolved in a little cold water, 1 cupful of raisins, seeded and chopped, 1 of currants, 1 teaspoonful of all kinds of spices, flour to roll.—[Mrs. A. G. Guyer.

GOOD DOUGHNUTS.—While the doughnut question is being agitated, I'll send in my ideas concerning them, also my recipe. I have tried all kinds of recipes and am thoroughly convinced that too much shortening and fat that is not real hot are the principal causes for their soaking fat. I have found one that is just right: 2 eggs, 1 cup sugar, 2-3 cup new milk (which contains about the right amount of shortening), 2 even teaspoonfuls cream of tartar, 1 even teaspoonful soda, flour enough to roll easily, salt and nutmeg. Have the fat real hot.—[Mrs. B. F. Crocker.

Pastry.

No flippant, sugared notion
Shall my appetite appease,
Or bate my soul's devotion
To apple pie and cheese.
—*Eugene Field.*

PASTRY.—1 pound butter, 1 pound flour, 1 teaspoonful salt; wash the butter, then sift the flour, adding the salt, take half the butter and mix into the flour with the hands, afterwards wetting it with ice water—use a knife for that purpose—make it soft but not sticky; put dough on a board and roll twice, making it an inch thick, roll up, and put in ice chest over night, also the other half of the butter; next morning put butter where it will soften, roll out the dough half an inch thick, and spread with the butter, repeating this twice, then roll up and put in a pan, placing where it can be chilled. It will then be ready for use.—[Mrs. E. F. Smith.

MINCE PIE MEAT.—2 quarts chopped meat, 1 quart suet, 3 1-2 quarts chopped apples, 1 1-2 cups chopped citron, 1 lemon, juice and grated peel, 4 teaspoonfuls vanilla, 3 cups raisins, currants, salt and sugar to taste, 2 teaspoonfuls clove, 3 teaspoonfuls nutmeg, 6 teaspoonfuls cinnamon, 1 teaspoonful allspice, 1 cup molasses, 1-2 cup brandy, 2 teaspoonfuls vinegar.—[M. P. C.

PUMPKIN PIE.—1 quart pumpkin, 1 quart milk, 1 1-3 cups sugar, 1 teaspoonful ginger, cinnamon and salt, 4 eggs, butter the size of an egg. Heat half of the milk and pour over pumpkin and spices; add cold milk and eggs last.—[Mrs. J. S. Nicholson.

SQUASH PIE.—1 pint squash cooked and sifted, 1 quart milk, 1 cup sugar, small piece butter, 1 teaspoonful ginger or cinnamon, little salt. Scald milk and pour over mixture, then add 3 eggs well beaten. Enough for 2 large pies.—[G. B. H.

SQUASH PIE WITHOUT EGGS.—1 1-2 cups squash, 1 small teaspoonful salt mixed into the squash, 1 quart milk, 6 crackers rolled fine, sugar to taste, 1 teaspoonful ginger, 1 teaspoonful cinnamon. This makes 2 pies.—[Mrs. J. W. Drew.

PINEAPPLE PIE.—1 can pineapple chopped fine, 1 1-4 cups sugar, 2 tablespoonfuls flour, 2 eggs, 1 1-2 cups of the juice. This makes 2 pies.—[Mrs. Chas. H. Carney.

CRANBERRY PIE.—2 cups cranberries chopped quite fine, 1 cup raisins chopped, 1 1-2 cups sugar, 2 tablespoonfuls cornstarch, 1 1-2 cups boiling water, 1 teaspoonful vanilla, small piece butter. Makes 3 pies.—[L. T. C.

CRANBERRY PIE.—1 quart berries chopped quite fine, 2 cups sugar, 1-2 cup molasses, 1 tablespoonful cornstarch dissolved in just a little cold water, to which add 1 1-2 cups boiling water. Bake with top crust. It makes, I think, 3 pies. Very good.
—[M. J. Hall.

LEMON PIE.—1 whole lemon grated, taking out seeds, 1 cup sugar, yolks of 3 eggs, 1 small teaspoonful salt, 1 large or 2 small potatoes grated. Turn on the potatoes 1 cup boiling water and add to the rest, well beaten. Frost with the white of the eggs, and brown. This makes 1 large pie.—[Mrs. J. W. Drew.

LEMON PIE.—3 lemons, 7 eggs, 2 1-2 cups sugar. Leave out the whites of 4 eggs and 1-2 cup sugar for frosting. Beat whites to a stiff froth. This makes 2 pies.—[Mrs. C. H. Eldridge.

LEMON PIE.—1 heaping tablespoonful cornstarch, mix with a little cold water, then add 1 teacup boiling water; set on the top of teakettle to cook; take a bowl, break in 2 eggs, and whip; add 1 cup sugar, juice and grated rind of 1 lemon, 1 tablespoonful melted butter, stir in cornstarch; make a nice crust. A nice pie.
—[Mrs. Emeline Bearse.

LEMON PIE.—2 lemons, 2 cups sugar, 5 eggs, 2 tablespoonfuls cornstarch, 1 pint milk ; grate the lemons, add the juice, stir together ; scald the cornstarch with milk. This will make 2 pies, which must be baked in rich puff paste.—[Mrs. John O'Neil.

RAISIN PIE.—1 cup raisins stoned and chopped fine, 1 tablespoonful flour mixed with raisins, juice of 1 lemon, 1 small cup water, 1 cup sugar. This makes 1 pie. Use top crust.

—[Mrs. C. A. Bursley.

RHUBARB PIE.—1 large coffee cup chopped rhubarb, 2 heaping teaspoonfuls cornstarch, 1 cup sugar, yolks of 2 eggs. Bake with one crust and frost with the whites.—[Mrs. C. E. Harris.

TART SHELLS.—1 cup lard and butter. 1 tablespoonful white sugar, white of 1 egg, 3 tablespoonfuls cold water, flour to make stiff paste, roll out. Cut with a round cutter.

LEMON CHEESE.—1-4 pound butter, 1 pound sugar, 6 eggs, rind of 2 lemons and juice of 3. Put all the ingredients into a saucepan, carefully grating the lemon rind and straining the juice. Keep stirring the mixture over the fire until the sugar is dissolved and it begins to thicken ; when of the consistency of honey it is done. Make tart shells of rich pastry and fill with the cheese.

—[Mrs. E. S. Bradford.

Puddings and Light Desserts.

The proof of the pudding is the eating.
—*Cervantes.*

INDIAN PUDDING.—3 tablespoonfuls meal, 1 tablespoonful flour, 2 eggs, 3-4 cup molasses, 1 quart milk, 1-2 teaspoonful salt, 1-2 teaspoonful ginger, 1-2 cup suet. Scald the milk in a double boiler, mix the meal and flour with a little cold milk and put it in the hot milk, stirring constantly until it thickens, then pour into a pudding dish with the molasses, eggs, etc., and bake two or three hours in a moderate oven. 1 or 2 sweet apples sliced fine and mixed with it improve it very much.—[Mrs. J. S. Nicholson.

HARTFORD PUDDING.—1-2 loaf or pieces of stale cake, pour over 1 wineglass of wine; beat 3 eggs with 3 tablespoonfuls sugar and pour on them 1 pint boiling milk; pour over cake, beat well, steam in a mould 1 1-2 hours.—[Mrs. Wm. P. Lewis.

PRUNE PUDDING.—1 pound prunes, whites 4 eggs, 1 cup sugar; cook prunes day before, draining the liquor; cut in small pieces in pudding dish; beat eggs to stiff froth, stir in cup of sugar and put into the prunes; beat all together. Bake twenty minutes or half hour.—[Miss Flora Hallett.

SNOW PUDDING.—1 box Cox's gelatine dissolved in 1 pint cold water, afterwards pour in 1 pint boiling water, then flavor with 1 teaspoonful lemon extract, stand it in a cool place until it begins to jellify; in the meantime take the whites of 8 eggs, beat stiff, then take the jelly and beat both together thoroughly until you are sure that the two will not separate when put away to harden; then take the yolks of the 8 eggs, mix with 1 cup sugar; have 1 quart milk boiling in a double boiler, then stir in the eggs and sugar; stir it until it begins to thicken, then let it cool, and flavor with a teaspoonful of lemon extract. The white part must be stiff so it

can be cut, then pour the yellow sauce over it. This is very nice.
—[Miss Rebecca E. Blau.

FIG PUDDING.—1 cupful suet, 1 pound figs, 3 eggs, 2 cupfuls bread crumbs, 1 cupful sugar, 2 cupfuls milk. Wash, pick over the figs, and chop; chop the suet; beat the eggs light without separating; mix all the ingredients thoroughly, turn into a well-greased mould, cover and boil three hours. Serve hot.
—[Mrs. Lot Crocker.

QUEEN OF PUDDINGS.—1 pint nice bread crumbs, 1 quart milk, 1 cup sugar, yolks of 4 eggs, grated rind of 1 lemon, piece of butter size of egg cut in small pieces and put on top. Bake like custard; when baked spread over the top the whites of the eggs beaten to a stiff froth with 1 cup sugar and juice of 1 lemon. Brown lightly in oven. Real nice.—[Mrs. J. R. Hall.

GEN. HANCOCK PUDDING.—3 cups flour, 1 coffee cup chopped raisins, 1-2 cup dried currants, 1 teacup suet chopped fine, 1-2 cup molasses, 1-2 cup sugar, 2 cups sweet milk, 1 teaspoonful soda, little salt. Mix, and steam three hours. Sauce: 1 cup sugar, 1 egg beaten very light, 1-2 cup hot milk.—[Mrs. Geo. Penniman.

LEMON PUDDING.—6 crackers rolled fine, yolks of 6 eggs, 2 cups sugar, grated rind and juice of 2 lemons, 1 pint milk, 1 small cup butter. Soak the crackers in the milk. Frosting: The whites of 6 eggs beaten to a stiff froth and 3 tablespoonfuls sugar. Then set back in the oven to brown.—[Mrs. E. E. Field.

SPONGE PUDDING.—4 tablespoonfuls flour, 4 tablespoonfuls sugar, yolks of 4 eggs, 1 quart milk, a little salt. Stir the milk scalding hot into the flour, sugar, and yolks of eggs. When ready to put in oven add the whites beaten stiff and fold them in. Bake one-half hour and serve immediately. Serve with foamy sauce, flavored with sherry wine.—[Mrs. George F. Baker.

Wedding...
...Stationery

WE are prepared at all times to fill orders for wedding invitations, reception invitations and cards. We employ the best copper plate engravers in Boston and New York, and can give results that no young lady need be ashamed of (the kind of work we are proud to claim with our imprint).

If a lower priced grade of work is desired, our imitation of plate printing is unsurpassed, and we can give you the latest styles in shapes, finish and tints.

VISITING CARDS.

ADDRESS CARDS,

CAKE BOXES,

JAP. NAPKINS,

WAXED PAPER,

or anything you may need in the printing line can be secured of us.

F. B. & F. P. GOSS,

Pleasant Street,   HYANNIS.

Sponge Pudding.—1-2 cup sugar, 1 cup milk, 1 pint flour, 1 egg, little salt, teaspoonful yeast powder. Steam one hour.
—[Mrs. K. R. Bearse.

Snowball Pudding.—2 tablespoonfuls cornstarch dissolved in a little cold water; add a pint of boiling water, beat the whites of 4 eggs stiff and beat into the cornstarch after removing from the fire; add a pinch of salt; put in cups to cool. Take yellow and beat in 2-3 cup sugar, 1 teaspoonful cornstarch, put into a quart of boiling milk, let it thicken up, and remove from the stove; flavor to taste. Drop the balls into the custard.
—[Mrs. Osborn Crowell.

Moonshine Pudding.—Whites of 6 eggs beaten very stiff, beat into this 6 tablespoonfuls powdered sugar, take 1 cup fruit and stir in. Pack with ice until wanted. Eat with sweetened cream; vanilla.—[Mrs. E. O. Bond.

Cheap Fruit Pudding.—1 cup molasses, 1 cup milk, 2 eggs, 1-2 cup melted butter, 1 cup raisins, 1 cup currants, small piece citron, 3 cups flour, salt, spice to taste, teaspoonful powder or cream of tartar and soda. Put the batter in a tight covered pail, set in water, steam nearly three hours.—[S. L. H.

Rice Pudding.—Cook in a double boiler 1-2 cup rice in 1 pint water until the water has all cooked away, then add 1 quart milk and cook one hour. Beat together 1 cup sugar, 3 eggs, 2 teaspoonfuls salt; stir this into the rice and add raisins and a little nutmeg. Turn into a buttered pudding dish and bake about thirty minutes in a slow oven.—[Mrs. A. G. Guyer.

Rice Pudding.—1 quart milk, 3 tablespoonfuls rice, 1-2 cup sugar, 1-2 teaspoonful cinnamon or nutmeg, butter the size of a small egg.—[Mrs. Lizzie C. Johnson.

Cerealine Pudding.—2 quarts skim milk, 5 cups cerealine, 1 1-2 cups molasses, and a little salt. Bake very slowly four hours or more, stirring occasionally, and adding more cold milk as it cooks away. Similar to an Indian pudding. Serve with butter or cream.—[Mrs. G. E. Tillson.

COTTAGE PUDDING.—1 cup milk, 1-2 cup sugar, 1 egg, 2 tablespoonfuls melted butter, 1 1-2 teaspoonfuls baking powder sifted with 1 pint flour; add 1-2 cup raisins seeded and chopped. Bake slowly one-half hour. Serve with sauce. Sauce: 1 pint boiling water, 1 cup sugar, thicken with 4 teaspoonfuls flour; cook about five minutes; strain, add a piece of butter the size of a walnut and flavoring.—[Mrs. Minnie L. Snow.

LEMON SAUCE.—2 cups hot water, 1 cup sugar, 3 heaping teaspoonfuls cornstarch, tablespoonful butter, flavor.
—[Mrs. George F. Crocker.

FRENCH TOAST.—1 baker's loaf of bread sliced in inch slices; make a batter of 6 eggs and 1 quart milk, soak three hours; fry in butter brown. To be eaten warm with cold sauce. Very good.
—[Mrs. W. A. Hallett.

APPLE FRITTERS.—Beat 2 eggs without separating until light, add 1-2 pint milk, 1-2 teaspoonful salt, sufficient flour to make a thin batter that will pour from a spoon; pare and chop (not fine) 2 good-sized apples, mix these into the batter, and add 2 teaspoonfuls baking powder; mix and drop by spoonfuls into smoking hot fat; when brown turn. Take out with skimmer and drain on brown paper. Serve very hot, dusted with powdered sugar.
—[Mrs. George W. Hallett.

BANANA FRITTERS.—1 cup flour, 1-4 cup sugar, 1 teaspoonful baking powder, 2 eggs, little salt. Beat all together, add sliced bananas, drop in hot lard with teaspoon.—[Mrs. Geo. F. Crocker.

POPOVERS.—1 cup milk, 1 cup flour, 1 egg, salt. Bake in cups. Serve with sauce.—[Mrs. Wm. P. Lewis.

LEMON SAUCE.—1 cup sugar, 1-4 cup water, 1 teaspoonful butter, 1 teaspoonful lemon juice. Boil sugar and water until it thickens slightly, add butter and lemon juice; serve as soon as butter is melted. Serve with wafers.—[Mrs. George F. Crocker.

BANANA CREAM.—1 1-2 pints of milk on the stove to scald. Beat together 1-2 cupful of sugar, 1 tablespoonful of cornstarch, yolks of 4 eggs, and add to the milk when it is hot, stir until it thickens, but do not let it boil. Slice 4 bananas thin, 1-3 cupful sugar over them. Turn on the custard and sprinkle cocoanut on the top.—[Mrs. Chas. H. Carney.

COFFEE CREAM.—Soak half a box of gelatine for two hours in 1 cup of cold water. Put half a cupful of the best coffee, finely ground, into a pint of boiling milk and let it stand five minutes, then strain the milk through a thick cloth upon a cupful of sugar, and add to it the well beaten yolks of 4 eggs. Stir the whole over the fire until creamy, then take from the fire and add the gelatine. Stir the gelatine well, and pour the cream through a soup strainer, set away in a cool place; when it begins to thicken stir briskly into it a pint of whipped cream and turn into a wet mould.
—[Miss Carrie L. Crowell.

CHOCOLATE BLANC MANGE.—3 cups milk, 1-2 cup sugar, 2 squares Baker's chocolate, 3 (heaping) spoonfuls cornstarch. Boil milk, add cornstarch and sugar, cook well, stirring all the time. Melt chocolate on teakettle, add to milk and cornstarch, stir hard, flavor.—[Mrs. Geo. W. Hallett.

FLOATING ISLANDS.—1 quart milk and boil, 1-2 dozen eggs beaten stiff, dip into boiling milk and remove; put into a dish; beat the yolks with 1 cup sugar and stir into the boiling milk to thicken, remove and put over whites which are beaten.
—[Mrs. Wm. Sherman.

STRAWBERRY CUSTARD.—Make a custard of 1 quart milk and

yolks of 5 eggs, sweeten to taste. A gill of sugar and pint of ripe strawberries, crush together and pass through a strainer. Take whites of eggs, and while beating to a stiff froth add a gill of sugar, little at a time; then to sugar and eggs add the strawberry juice. Serve with custard.—[Mrs. O. H. Crowell.

FRUIT JELLY.—3-4 of a box of gelatine dissolved in 1-2 pint cold water one hour, then add 1-2 pint of boiling water, the juice of 2 lemons and 2 cups of sugar, strain and let it stand until it begins to thicken, then stir in fruit and nuts cut in small pieces. This will make two moulds. Serve with whipped cream.

—[Mrs. Minnie L. Snow.

FRUIT JELLY.—Cut 6 bananas in lengthwise slices, slice 6 oranges, dissolve a little more than 1-2 box Cox's gelatine in 1-2 pint cold water, then add 1-2 pint boiling water, the juice of 2 or 3 lemons, and sweeten to taste. In any vegetable dish place a layer of the cut bananas, then a layer of the sliced oranges, sprinkle a little sugar over them. Fill the dish in this order, when the gelatine has cooled a little pour it over the bananas and oranges, and set away to harden. Turn out of the mould and serve very cold.—[Mrs. Obed Baxter.

JELLIED PRUNES.—Soak 1-2 box of gelatine in 1-2 cup cold water. Cook 1-2 pound prunes until soft in 1 quart of cold water. When they are done drain them and cut in pieces, and pour the hot prune water over the gelatine, adding 1 cup of granulated sugar, rind and juice of 1-2 a lemon. Serve with whipped cream.

—[Mrs. E. E. Field.

STRAWBERRY JELLY.—Soak 1 box of gelatine in 1-2 pint cold water twenty minutes, add 1 pint boiling water, stir until dissolved, add scant half pint sugar, strained juice of 1 1-2 pints of strawberries, and juice of 1 lemon. Strain and cool.

—[Mrs. E. E. Field.

PINEAPPLE AND ORANGES.—Cut off the top of the pineapple, pare away the bottom so it may stand firm, then with a spoon scoop out the pulp, leaving the shell whole. Cut the pulp into small pieces and mix with 3 oranges cut in small pieces, sweeten, put in a jar and pack in ice and salt, let stand for two hours; when frozen and ready to serve turn mixture into pineapple shell, garnish dish around the shell with leaves from the top of the pineapple, serve with whipped cream. Very dainty.—[J. B. C.

BANANA CHARLOTTE.—Line a mould with slices of banana, soak 1-4 box gelatine in 1-4 cup cold water, then dissolve in 1-4 cup boiling water, add 1 cup sugar and juice of 1 lemon, strain through cheese cloth and add pulp of 2 bananas cut in slices; stir the mixture over ice-cold water until it begins to thicken, then beat in the whites of 3 eggs well beaten, until dry; when the charlotte becomes stiff as a sponge cake batter turn into lined mould and let stand until thoroughly cold and set. Serve with whipped cream or boiled custard of the yolk of the eggs. Oranges may be used in place of bananas; line the mould with quarters and add 1 cup of pulp and juice in the charlotte. Excellent.—[J. B. C.

MOUSSE.—1 quart thick cream; add to a scant cup of powdered sugar 1-2 pint black coffee or fruit juice, place dish in ice water and whip to froth; skim off froth and whip the thin again. Pour carefully into freezer and leave three or four hours packed in ice and salt.—[Mrs. Franklin Crocker.

ICE CREAM.—1 can condensed milk, 2 cans of cream, 2 cans of hot water, 1-2 cup sugar, 2 or 3 eggs, flavor to taste. Beat eggs and sugar, add milk and cream, then hot water; scald, but do not boil.—[Mrs. Julius Howland.

ICE CREAM.—1 pint of cream, 1 pint of milk, 1 teaspoonful of gelatine dissolved in water. Sweeten and flavor to taste. Fine.
—[Sallie Hallett.

ICE CREAM.—1 cup cream, 2 cups milk, 1 small can condensed milk. Sweeten and flavor to taste.—[Mrs. Wm. J. Wyer.

93

Sweets to the Sweet.

STUFFED DATES.—Remove the stones of the dates and fill with the following : Beat the white of an egg with confectioner's sugar, have chopped fine the required amount of English walnuts or peanuts, mix the chopped nuts and egg and sugar together, and stuff the dates.—[Mrs. John C. Bearse.

STUFFED RAISINS.—Cut open choice raisins on one side and remove the seeds ; fill with bits of blanched almonds, English walnuts, or candied cherries ; close each raisin thus filled and wrap in another seeded raisin. Roll in fine granulated sugar.

CANDIED ALMONDS AND ENGLISH WALNUTS.—Boil 1 cup granulated sugar, 1-8 teaspoonful cream of tartar, and 3-4 cup of water over a very hot fire ; do not stir after the boiling has begun ; remove from fire as soon as there is a very faint yellow tinge to the syrup. Take the shelled nuts (almonds having been blanched) on the point of a large needle, dip them in syrup, then drop on oiled paper.

TO BLANCH ALMONDS.—Pour over boiling water and let them remain until the skins will remove easily.—[Mrs. Albert Bacon.

FONDANT.—Place a porcelain basin over the fire in a pan of water ; dissolve in it 2 cupfuls granulated sugar, 1 cupful boiling water, 1 teaspoonful vinegar, a pinch of cream of tartar, and cook all together twelve minutes. Do not stir ; test by dropping a little in cold water ; when it congeals into a soft ball it is ready to pour onto a plate to cool. Do not scrape the pan. When cool enough to handle stir one way only, and then put away for twenty-four hours ; it is then ready to mould into candies. If it should have a tendency to stick, work in raw sugar. It can be flavored as desired, when moulding. For a pretty variety, stone some dates, fill the cavities with the cream, cut the dates into small pieces and cover with cream. One may conceal in the fondant candied fruits, nut meats, figs, fresh fruits.

PANOCHE.—Boil together 2 pounds of brown sugar and a cupful of milk until the mixture hardens when dropped into cold water. Add to this a pound or more of chopped walnuts, a piece of butter size of an egg, and a teaspoonful vanilla.—[L. F. H.

FUDGE.—2 cups sugar, 2 squares chocolate, 1-2 cup cream (or milk), small piece butter (size of walnut), teaspoonful of vanilla. Boil fifteen minutes without stirring; remove from fire and beat until it begins to thicken. Turn out to cool.

—[Mrs. F. W. Kingman.

FUDGE.—2 cups sugar, 2-3 cup milk (or cream better), butter size of an egg, chocolate to suit, say 2 squares; add nuts or figs or dates, or anything else desired. Cook until it forms a soft ball in water; take off and beat until it nearly sugars, and pour in cooling pan. Can be made in chafing dish. Cocoa may be used instead of chocolate; use 2 tablespoonfuls.—[E. C. Wheeler.

VANILLA TAFFY.—1 cup vinegar, 3 cups sugar, butter size of a walnut, 1-2 teaspoonful vanilla.—[Miss Fanny A. Snow.

BUTTER SCOTCH.—3 cups sugar, 3-4 cup water, butter size of a walnut, a pinch of soda, flavor to suit the taste. When cooling mark off into squares with a knife.—[Miss Fanny A. Snow.

BUTTER SCOTCH.—1 cup butter, 1 cup brown sugar, 1 cup molasses. Boil until hard in water, from ten to twenty minutes. Turn on buttered tins and score.—[Mrs. E. O. Bond.

CHOCOLATE CARAMELS.—2 cups sugar, 1 cup milk, 1-4 pound chocolate. Boil in frying pan twenty minutes, add 1-2 cup butter, boil four minutes, take from fire, stir until just before it turns to sugar.—[Mrs. E. O. Bond.

A SIMPLE SYRUP.—To 1 cup water add 2 cups granulated sugar. Remove the instant it begins to boil.—[Peter Pineo Chase.

Wrinkles.

TABLE OF MEASURES AND WEIGHTS.—

1 quart of flour = 1 pound.
2 cupfuls of butter = 1 pound.
1 generous pint of liquid = 1 pound.
2 cupfuls of granulated sugar = 1 pound.
2 heaping cupfuls of powdered sugar = 1 pound.
1 pint of finely chopped meat packed solidly = 1 pound.

—[Miss Barry.

A principle which the IVANOUGH COOK BOOK strongly advocates is the use of pure baking powders. "The only pure baking powders are made from cream of tartar in which are combined the most useful leavening agencies and healthful food qualities. In imitation powders alum is used, which is poisonous and seriously affects the health." To this matter our ladies should give attention—the difference in price between the cheap powders and the pure, best powders not being worthy of consideration.

To CLEAN SILVER.—To 1 gallon of soft water add piece of washing soda size of an egg. Place silver in clean agate kettle with soda water enough to cover and set over fire and let boil fifteen minutes; take from kettle and rinse immediately in hot soap suds and dry on clean towel.—[G. B. H.

To DO UP SHIRT BOSOMS.—Take 2 ounces of fine white gum-arabic powder, put it in a pitcher and pour in a pint of water; having covered it, let it stand all night; in the morning pour it carefully from the dregs into a bottle, cork it, and keep it for use. A tablespoonful of gum water poured in a pint of starch made in the usual manner will give to lawn, either white or printed, a look of newness.—[Mrs. M. L. Bearse.

Melted parafine poured over jellies and jams is the surest safe-guard against air.

Beeswax and salt will make rusty flatirons as clean and smooth as glass.

Table cloths should be frequently altered in the folding for iron-ing. This prevents their wearing at the crease. They may be folded double part of the time and then in triple folds.

To STONE RAISINS.—Put them in a dish and pour boiling water over them ; cover and let them remain in it ten minutes. It will soften them so that by rubbing each raisin between the thumb and finger, the seeds will come out clean. Then they are ready for cut-ting or chopping if required.

Lay sardines on tissue paper to free them from oil.

Salt will curdle new milk. Hence in preparing dishes from the latter, add salt after it is taken from the fire.

Never keep a furiously hot fire ; a gentle and sustained heat is always best.

If you are troubled with ants, ask your druggist for a strong so-lution of corrosive sublimate ; wipe your shelves with it and they will disappear. This is unfailing.

TO OUR READERS.

It is regretted that owing to the limited number of pages, which the committee was not allowed to exceed, all the excellent recipes contributed could not have been embodied in this book.

A number of recipes given by former residents are appreciated.

We would call the attention of our patrons to the advertisements that appear on these pages. Let us show these firms our appreci-ation by giving them, in return, our patronage.

www.ingramcontent.com/pod-product-compliance
Lightning Source LLC
Chambersburg PA
CBHW021409090426
42742CB00009B/1073